Old
Wigtownshire

Jack Hunter

The importance of the lifeboat is emphasised by the coastal cargo schooner with which it is sharing Port Logan Harbour, a reminder that for centuries the main form of transport in the South Rhinns was by sea. In the background the features of the Thomas Telford-designed, Colonel McDowall-financed harbour are fully displayed. The curved breakwater of boulders on the left gives way on the right to a pier of roughly dressed stone. The latter terminates in Port Logan's best known feature, the little, granite lighthouse beloved of artists and photographers. Not only attractive but keeper-friendly, it contains a fireplace and a latrine. Sadly a dispute between Laird McDowall of Logan and the Northern Lighthouse Commissioners over the cost of maintaining this little gem led to its going out of use with consequent major loss of trade for the harbour and eventual dereliction.

Stenlake Publishing Ltd

© 2014 Jack Hunter
First Published in the United Kingdom, 2014
Stenlake Publishing Limited
54-58 Mill Square, Catrine, KA5 6RD
www.stenlake.co.uk

ISBN 9781840336603

Printed by
Blissetts, Roslin Road, Acton, W3 8DH

Wigtownshire and especially the Rhinns have always been well known as a stronghold of Clydesdale horse breeding and the McFarlane family of Salchrie Farm between Stranraer and Kirkcolm were prominent exponents along with names like the Marshalls of Bridgebank and James Hunter of Whiteleys. The name of McFarlane figures prominently in the catalogues for Wigtown Show in the late 1940s. This Clydesdale horse had every reason to look pensive for the internal combustion engine powering the float behind it spelled the end of the heavy horse as the principal source of motive power on the farm and the road. However Clydesdale breeding still flourishes in Wigtownshire and not solely out of sentiment because a good market for the breed still exists in North America.

FURTHER READING

In compiling this publication I have referred to numerous works, many of them out of print. For reasons of space, only the main ones are listed below although others are mentioned in the text. I am happy to acknowledge my indebtedness to all the authors I have consulted, whether named or not. Please note that none of the following titles is available from Stenlake Publishing.

Agnew, Sir Andrew *Wigtownshire; An Illustrated Guide for Visitors* 1908

Donnachie, Ian *The Industrial Archaeology of Galloway* 1971

Gifford, John *The Buildings of Scotland: Dumfries and Galloway* 1996

Hutchinson, F. *Tours in Galloway; Official Guide to the PPWJR* 1901

McLay, Jas *The Douglas-Ewart High School* 1994

MacQueen, John *Place Names of the Wigtownshire Moors and Machars* 2008

M'Ilwraith, Wm *The Visitors' Guide to Wigtownshire* 1875

Marshall, Mike (ed.) *Around Us the Waves* 2010

Miller, Peter *Galloway Shipwrecks* 1992

Smith, John *Cheesemaking in Scotland; A History* 1995

Thorne, H.D. *Rails to Portpatrick* 1976

Todd, Wm *The Parish of Kirkmaiden* 1854

The (New) Statistical Account of Scotland 1841

The Third Statistical Account of Scotland 1965

Dfs, Kbt, and Wigtown Trades' Directory 1928

INTRODUCTION

Located in the extreme south-west corner of Scotland, Wigtownshire today is a remote, isolated, peripheral region. However this has been the case only since the nineteenth century and the coming of the railway and later of the internal combustion engine. For the previous millennia the main form of transport had been by sea and in that situation the county was at the heart of the west coast national communications network, at a crossroads where the international Euroroute up the Irish Sea met on the east the seaway along the Solway coast into northern England and on the west the highway up Belfast Lough into Ulster. And the physical geography of Wigtownshire ensured that its location had maximum impact, for the former county of approximately 480 square miles has over 130 miles of coastline with nowhere more than thirteen miles from the sea. Consequently every race or culture which came to Scotland came, and came early, to Wigtownshire.

The western and eastern shores of Luce Bay are dotted with the scanty traces of Scotland's first known inhabitants, the nomadic hunter gatherers of the Mesolithic period with evidence that they moved inland, for example up the Bladnoch and Tarff rivers to the area of Barlae. Their farming successors of the Neolithic age built their great ceremonial stadia at Dunragit and massive tombs up the Luce valley. The Celts around the time of the birth of Jesus covered parts of the landscape with their villages of round houses, their crannogs,

and even the odd broch. Their Roman would-be conquerors of 80AD bequeathed to us a fortlet on the River Bladnoch near the village of that name. A wooden Anglo-Saxon cathedral complex stood at Whithorn and the sculptors in its workshops created a cluster of the famous ninth century Whithorn crosses, one of them now in the church at Kirkinner close to its original location. The Vikings on their journeys to their possessions in Man and Ireland made overnight stops here in order to maintain control over the vital sea routes. Names like Eggerness and Sinniness are their calling cards and places like The Wig at Kirkcolm and Larbrax Bay their former stopover locations. The latter still displays the triple banks and ditches used to protect their promontory camp site.

The last hostile invaders of Britain, the Normans, did not come directly to Wigtownshire but the Anglo-Norman grandsons of William the Conqueror's knights did arrive in the twelfth century at the behest of Scotland's King David I. In return for grants of land these newcomers used their military expertise and castle-building skills to maintain control over the independent-minded Gallovidians. The mottes (earthen mounds shaped like a plum pudding) on which their wooden castles stood can be comfortably viewed from the road at Druchtag just outside Mochrum, Boreland near Kirkcowan, Innermessan north of Stranraer on the A77, and Sandhead. If they seem rather small for their purpose, remember the effects of almost 1000 years of erosion.

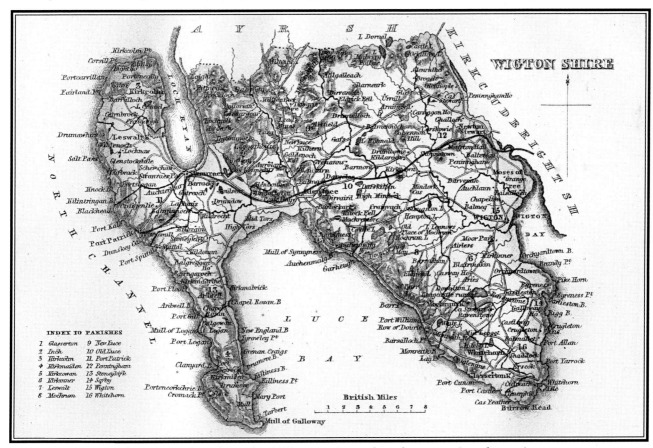

Map of Wigtownshire from the 1870s, at a time when the county's and town's names
were spelled without the second w.

3

But the most influential, pervasive, and lasting marine link was the one established with another member of the Irish Sea province. For Ireland is only 21 miles from Wigtownshire across the North Channel, the crossing from Portpatrick to Donaghadee being the shortest route between the British mainland and Ireland. Links with that country were well-established by 5,000 years ago: two separate collections of pieces of Antrim flint have been found near Portpatrick. They were either the pack of a travelling Irish merchant trading the raw material for making weapons and tools or the stock of an itinerant Irish flint worker of around 3,000 BC. The link has continued through the seventeenth century plantation of Ulster, the famine-induced large-scale migrations of the nineteenth century and the potato-lifting squads (the tattie howkers) of the twentieth, to the present when Ulsterbus have a depot in Stranraer and farmers, business people, and members of the professions form a sizeable and welcome part of the local population. In easy visual confirmation of the close Wigtownshire-Ireland connection, visitors to Portpatrick should not be surprised to walk along St. Patrick Street or to see the Mount Stewart hotel.

However the corollary of the Shire's strong links by sea with its various Irish Sea neighbours is the tenuousness of the link with central Scotland and the centres of power. The topography of southern Scotland makes communication between Wigtownshire and Edinburgh difficult even today, a fact which previous local rulers exploited to political advantage. They also made effective use of their strategic position on the exposed flanks of both Scotland and England to play off one kingdom against the other and had no compunction about changing sides. In the Wars of Independence Wigtownshire's most powerful chief, Dugald MacDouall of Logan, sided with King Edward against Robert the Bruce. When the latter's brothers Thomas and Alexander landed in Loch Ryan with a small force from Ireland in 1307, they were attacked and routed by MacDouall, who dispatched the brothers to Edward at Carlisle, where they were executed. This was in spite of the fact that in 1263, 40 years earlier, the MacDouall of the day and his followers had fought as part of the Scottish army at the Battle of Largs. All this created in Wigtownshire people a strongly independent and egalitarian spirit which arguably was displayed in the Covenanting times of the seventeenth century, the smuggling days of the early eighteenth, and is still very evident today.

Visitors to the area are always surprised to see plants growing happily in the open which in other areas require the shelter of greenhouse or conservatory, often being classed as indoor species. For this exotic feature of the local scene the sea is again responsible. The shape of Wigtownshire means that the usual moderating influence of sea on climate is greatly strengthened and the presence of a branch of the Gulf Stream (North Atlantic Drift) running up the west coast increases the effect. Consequently the former county is famed for its mild winters with minimal frost and snow, hospitable conditions for natives of warmer climes, especially Australia and New Zealand. Logan Botanic Garden is the best known location for experiencing the disorientating effect of Wigtownshire's thoroughly atypical flora.

The mild climate and the relatively high rainfall brought from the Atlantic by the prevailing westerlies make ideal conditions for grass to grow enthusiastically for a very long season, as reluctant gardeners know to their cost However the gardener's loss is the farmer's gain: thanks to its lush pastures Wigtownshire is one of the most important areas in Scotland for dairy farming although the traditional Ayrshire cow has largely given way to the incomer Holstein. Another agricultural consequence of the mild maritime climate is that it favours the cultivation of early potatoes, which often can be harvested before their more celebrated Ayrshire counterparts.

Finally, an important effect of the sea on Wigtownshire life has been the creation of employment. The abundance of fish in the surrounding waters has given excellent opportunities for the development of a substantial industry but nature's bounty in this respect has been largely spurned. In the words of the Kirkmaiden minister in the 1841 *(New) Statistical Account:* "Fishing is not followed after with that industry and enterprise which the favourable locality would lead one to expect. Few make it their regular occupation."

The other maritime occupation of seafaring, however, has proved enduringly popular In 1841. enough seafarers lived in Kirkcolm parish for the sailors' ball to be a feature of the winter social calendar. while in his autobiography *Master in Sail* Captain James Learmonth observes of the Port William of his boyhood: "The village had for its size a very large community of sailors. It was possible to meet almost any day shipmasters, mates, second mates, apprentices and sailors young and old, home from the sea." Of Isle of Whithorn and its hinterland it is said in a recent book, *Around Us the Waves,* that about 1900 the residents included 50 holders of masters' certificates. Captain Learmonth was one of the last men to command a commercial, ocean-going, sailing ship. Other noteworthy seafarers from the area include Arctic explorer Sir John Ross from near Kirkcolm; Samuel Robinson of Kirkinner, who claimed in his autobiography to be the only man alive who had served an apprenticeship to the slave trade; and Admiral Sir Frederick Dalrymple Hamilton of Cairnryan, captain of *HMS Rodney* in one of the most famous engagements of the Second World War.

Thanks to the sea, Wigtownshire in its past and present is a unique part of Scotland and perhaps this book will convey something of that quality.

ACKNOWLEDGEMENTS

Over the years many people have shared their knowledge of Wigtownshire with me. I am grateful and heavily indebted to them. However any factual errors and all opinions and conclusions are entirely my responsibility.

"Mull of Galloway" Lighthouse

Perched over 200 feet above sea level on top of precipitous cliffs, the Mull of Galloway Lighthouse crowns the most southerly tip of Scotland in a latitude (54° 39' N) south of that of the city of Durham. Built in 1828 by Robert Stevenson, grandfather of the celebrated writer Robert Louis of that ilk, and visible from 25 miles, it provided much needed assistance to mariners by signalling the location of the fearsome tangle of tides and currents off the headland. Local tradition claims that nature anticipated the Northern Lighthouse Board. A seventeenth century author reported that at night passing sailors could see "a great light" coming from the Mull, the source reputedly being a rock of diamonds. A possible explanation is that the rock was actually a large rock crystal situated close to a feature, the Diamond Cave, just north of Gallie Craig, Sadly an eighteenth century French privateer saw the rock glittering in the sun, cut it out, and bore it off in vain hope of riches.

In 1895 the Mull of Galloway Lighthouse acquired a foghorn. With its signal of two quick blasts every 60 seconds it must have proved a noisy neighbour for the famous resident flocks of seabirds. The foghorn still occupies its vertiginous site but like all others of its kind is silent now. However, past generations of seafarers had more than natural hazards to contend with when passing Mull Head for it was a favoured resort of Kirkmaiden's notorious witches. From this vantage point they would cast spells on passing boats to destroy sailors who had antagonised them. Once a witch operating single-handed wove together the nine tides off the headland to entrap the vessel of a sailor who had offended. However, the task took longer than estimated for and although it was successfully completed, no time was left to disentangle the tides; this we are assured, is the cause of today's maelstrom of currents, races, and whirlpools.

The most southerly village in Scotland and the largest settlement in the most southerly parish, Drummore nestles on the sheltered eastern slope of the "great ridge" which gives it its Gaelic name. With a small bay providing a natural harbour, the site's advantages were obvious from an early date: flint tools and working debris show our Stone Age ancestors lived here thousands of years ago. The twelfth century motte close to High Drummore farmhouse and the sixteenth century tower house, now totally disappeared, on the site occupied today by Low Drummore farm buildings testify to the enduring appeal and importance of the area. However, this view is of the later part of the village seen from the west and featuring the houses along the modern road to Stranraer. Fittingly the two most prominent features of the scene are the harbour and what is now the parish church, for maritime and religious factors have played a key role in the history of the village and parish.

Kirkmaiden parish has many of the characteristics of an island and an island way of life for it is linked to the Rhinns Peninsula by a tenuous one-and-a-half mile wide isthmus, has over twenty miles of coastline, and the nearest station is seventeen miles away at Stranraer or Dunragit. Consequently until well after the First World War and the advent of the age of the internal combustion engine, the dominant form of transport was by sea. Drummore, with its natural harbour extended by a jetty was the communications hub. The pier was built around 1810 by a local farmer-*cum*-corn dealer almost inevitably called McDouall. A contemporary disparagingly described it as "but a kind of temporary erection". However improvements must have been effected for 100 years later it could accommodate vessels of 300 tons as well as the fortnightly Glasgow steamer. The remarkably attired gentleman in the foreground was, if a full-time fisherman, one of a small minority for in spite of abundant fish stocks few local people followed this occupation.

The vessels alongside the quay may be more modern but their purpose is the same, to deliver either coal or lime to the waiting row of horse-drawn farm carts or to load agricultural produce from them. In wartime visiting Drummore Harbour was not without its dangers even in the apparent safety of Luce Bay. In the early hours of a stormy November morning in 1917, a steamer, the *Main*, carrying a cargo of coal was attacked just off Drummore by a German U-boat and sunk by gunfire. Of the crew of fifteen only the captain survived, drifting for many hours in the waterlogged ship's boat until washed ashore late the next afternoon on the opposite side of Luce Bay near Monreith. Wearing no outdoor clothing, he owed his survival to the fact that his weight of twenty-two stones provided enough insulation to keep the cold at bay.

Mill Street, running down to the harbour, is the heart of Drummore. The large building in the left foreground, The Queen's Arms Hotel, is the biggest of its kind in the village. Like its kindred it enjoyed a golden age at the start of the twentieth century for according to a 1901 guide book the village was "steadily rising into favour as a seaside resort". And in her advert for the hotel in the same publication proprietrix Mrs Rankin modestly describes Drummore as a "splendid health resort". The small building on the right with the offset gable window was built by the district's biggest landowner, the Earl of Stair, as a community hall but is now demolished. The long building gable-on to the street, partly obscured by the Stair Hall, was the eighteenth century corn mill that gave the thoroughfare its name. It was water-powered courtesy of the Drummore Burn with a mill dam high up on the ridge at distant Damnaglaur. Like its neighbour it is also now demolished.

Church or Stair Street, the modern road into Drummore from the north, is appropriately dominated by the present parish, formerly United Free, church for Christianity in Kirkmaiden Parish has deep roots as the number of chapel and holy well sites testifies. Particularly important and perhaps of fifth century origin is the spectacularly inaccessible St. Medan's cave-chapel just north of the Mull of Galloway. Nineteenth century religion in Kirkmaiden is dominated by the remarkable figure of William Todd, parish schoolmaster for forty years until deposed for his allegiance to the new Free Church at the 1843 Disruption. A formidable champion of the new body, he conducted a prolonged and acrimonious debate with the parish minister in the correspondence columns of the local paper until told that further communications would be accepted only if paid for as advertisements. He also found time to pursue antiquarian interests, write a detailed and comprehensive history of the parish, and make stone sundials and wooden globes. He was the architect of the first Free Church building, now the church hall, across the road from its successor.

The Ship Hotel at the south end of Shore Street boasts an impressive sign. This is the oldest part of the village and the Ship was advantageously situated, for Shore Street is close to the harbour and on the original road north from the village. The houses in the right background show the line of the later road north along Church Street. In 1839 the hotel was one of ten licensed premises in Kirkmaiden Parish, a number which caused the local minister considerable unhappiness: "...their influence on the morals and comfort of the people is most pernicious". The situation had not improved by 1854 when local historian William Todd acidly pointed out that Drummore village had eight "whiskey shops" but was unable to support even one baker. Today Shore Street is no longer a through road, having been blocked by subsidence at its north end.

We intrude on the contestants at Drummore bowling club at a tense moment, when measurements are being taken to establish which bowl is nearest the target jack. The green is situated in Church Street close to the church (would William Todd have approved ?). The attire of participants and onlookers, particularly the headgear of the bowlers and the parasols of the spectating ladies seated on the right, suggests the picture was taken quite soon after the club's foundation in 1907. From 1928 the village also possessed a tennis club, which flourished for many years, being one of only two in the county to possess three courts. Sadly it is no more but the bowling club is still very much in existence. One of the houses on the seaward side of Church Street bears the regretful but honest name 'Nae View'.

Unflatteringly described in an 1847 gazetteer as "a crazy, disagreeable edifice", Drummore old parish church was begun in 1638, the year in which Scotland's National Covenant was signed, and is therefore often known as Kirk Covenant. The church bell, reused from secular purposes, dates from 1534. Kirk Covenant is still used for occasional religious services and community events. It was also the eighteenth century scene of an attempt by the minister, Mr Marshall, to eradicate the notorious Kirkmaiden witches. The entire adult congregation was ordered to report on a particular day, when the minister took his seat at a table in the centre of the church along with a witch hunter imported from distant Wigtown. As the congregation filed through the church, the witch hunter nudged the minister with her knee when any person emanated satanic symptoms. The list of names compiled in this way was not only large but included some of the parish's leading families. The document's subsequent accidental destruction by fire therefore eliminated much potential embarrassment.

In 1906 the Portpatrick and Wigtownshire Joint Committee, which operated the railway system in the south-west, decided to build a railway down the Rhinns Peninsula from Stranraer to Drummore. A detailed plan of the proposed route was prepared and still exists but the line was never built. Instead the committee bought two steam road motor cars at a cost of £1000 each to give Drummore a public transport link. In the first year, 1907, the service lost £550. This may be not unconnected with the facts that one of the two drivers had no experience of this type of vehicle and that the cars were ordered not to stop on steep hills. The discouraged Committee terminated the service but it was restarted in other hands, eventually being operated by the locally famous Murray family with their familiar blue buses. Proposals in 1898 and again in 1918 to build a Stranraer-Drummore railway came to nothing, Here one of the PWJC steam cars awaits passengers outside Stranraer's now vanished town station.

Now a farmhouse, Slockmill's name is a reminder of its industrial past. Powered by the waters of the Dam Burn, it may not have been a corn mill, for place names in the area suggest it could have been a scutching mill, part of the complex process of turning flax into linen. Kirkmaiden Parish has no great history of flax growing but neighbouring Stoneykirk was the most important area in Wigtownshire for linen production. In 1791 three mills for dressing linen and a bleachfield were recorded there. Both parishes were ideally situated to recruit skilled labour from Ulster. A short distance from Slockmill stands the Mull of Galloway Lighthouse's almost unknown little brother, the Crammag Head light. Automatic for its entire existence, it is no longer used. Sadly its construction meant the partial demolition of an earlier occupant of the headland, a circular, drystone, broch-type Iron Age structure of a type uncommon in the south-west.

With only two streets and a population in 1847 of 180 Port Logan is a community of modest size. But things might have been very different. In the early nineteenth century the government was anxious to improve communications on the short sea route between Britain and Ireland and Port Logan was one of the contenders for the role of Scottish terminal. Its case was supported by the most famous civil engineer of the day, Thomas Telford, who drew up plans to improve the harbour. However, Portpatrick won the day. Colonel Andrew McDowall (the later form of the family name) of Logan then built a modified version of Telford's plans and the new harbour won a modest share of the lucrative Irish cattle trade. The return cargo consisted of donkeys. The good times ended when the advent of steamers meant cattle could be shipped to English ports nearer their eventual destination. The hotel at the far end of Main Street was built by McDowall for the convenience of travellers as part of his harbour improvements

The most striking feature of Port Logan Main Street is that the houses stand on a much lower level than the roadway. The local explanation is that Colonel McDowall, concerned that the houses might be flooded in a gale, built a row of new houses, High Row, further up the hillside for the residents. However they chose not to move. To encourage a change of heart the Colonel then built an embankment in front of Main Street, obliterating the sea view. The residents still would not move, in some cases adding a second storey to their houses to retain the view. An alternative, villain-free possibility is that the houses were originally built behind the shelter of a bank of shingle thrown up by the sea. McDowall consolidated the shingle bank and built on it the new road to the improved harbour, in the process giving Main Street residents greater protection from storms.

THE HIGH ROW, PORT LOGAN.

According to the parish minister in 1839, the neat appearance of houses like those in Port Logan's High Row was deceptive for internally the cleanliness of the local houses left much to be desired. Rev. John Lamb also furnished particulars of the diet of the occupants. It seemed to consist of milk (when available), oatmeal porridge, potatoes, and herring or other varieties of fish. "Bread" took the form of oatcakes or potato and oatmeal scones. The minister deplored the recent appearance on local tables of tea and loaf bread but consoled himself with the thought that his parishioners' "attainments in religious knowledge are respectable and their general demeanour peaceful and orderly". Equally satisfactory to him was the fact that the smuggling, which had previously been the sole occupation of many of the leading residents of the parish, had now been completely abandoned.

A lifeboat station was established at Port Logan in 1866. The first boat was financed by money collected in Edinburgh by the well known writer of boys' stories R.M. Ballantyne and was consequently named *Edinburgh and R.M. Ballantyne*. The boat being dedicated here is unlikely to be that vessel but a later one, perhaps the *Frederick Allen* or the *Thomas McCunn*. The lifeboat house in the background is probably the new one built in 1907 on the site of the original building. When the station closed in 1926 the lifeboat house became the village hall and has remained so apart from a temporary metamorphosis into a school for the purposes of the BBC drama *Two Thousand Acres of Sky*, filmed largely in Port Logan a few years ago. The lifeboat crew can be seen at the front of the crowd on the left while a female VIP is seated on a bench on the minister's right.

Because Port Logan is a tidal harbour, a wooden carriage was required to launch and retrieve the lifeboat. The carriage was pulled by horses until the advent of the internal combustion engine and this caterpillar tractor. The ten or twelve oarsmen who propelled the lifeboat eventually became similarly redundant. The horses, and later the tractor, were also required to pull the lifeboat and carriage the mile across the narrow isthmus between Port Logan and New England Bay, thus extending the rescue coverage to Luce Bay. Multiple family membership of a lifeboat crew seems to have been a tradition in the service: thus in 1911 the Port Logan boat crew appropriately included four members of the Galloway family, one being the coxswain and one the second coxswain.

"One of the wonders of Galloway" according to a nineteenth-century guide, Logan Fishpond was constructed by enlarging a small, natural rock pool close to the shore to an impressive 160' circumference and 30' depth. The massive job was done in 1800 by French prisoners of war, who lived on a hulk in Drummore Harbour. The excavated stone was used in building the wall round the vegetable and fruit garden at Logan House nearby. The purpose of the fishpond, the brainchild of the already mentioned Colonel McDowall, was eminently practical: to provide fresh fish for the residents of Logan House whatever the season or weather. To this end the pond was stocked with several varieties of fish but mainly cod. A natural fissure was modified to link the pond with the sea, ensuring the water was changed while preventing the departure of the pond's occupants. No longer with a practical purpose, the pond today with its domesticated residents is an unusual and popular tourist attraction.

A private school existed in the Port Logan area in 1790. The master stayed with the parents of his pupils presumably without charge. By 1839 pupils were being taught English, writing, arithmetic, geography, and mathematics but the school fees had doubled to two shillings per quarter. The present building was erected as a result of the milestone Education Act of 1872,which introduced a national, state system of compulsory education, run by school boards. The school's slightly strange location at the opposite end of the bay from the village was possibly an attempt to find a reasonably central location for the entire catchment area with special emphasis on Logan estate and its large workforce. The school closed in the late 1950s after 78 years of existence.

Port Logan School, class of 1909. The similar age of all the pupils suggests this is one senior class and not the entire school population, a theory supported by the presence of only one teacher and the fact that in 1790 and 1839 before the introduction of compulsory education, the private school roll in the same village was around 40. The neatness of the pupils' dress reflects great credit on them and their parents while its variety testifies to their ingenuity. It is statistically likely that one of the boys in the group became a ship's captain for during its lifetime the school produced 37 boys who attained that elevated rank. The salary of the master must have exceeded the annual £3 paid to his 1790 predecessor.

Logan estate, home of a branch of the McDowall family from the late thirteen century until 1945, did not lack amenities. This generously proportioned duck pond was complemented by a curling pond, which in turn was complemented by a beech-floored curling rink The latter could be activated by spraying it with water in frosty weather, gas lights allowing play during the hours of darkness. Most important of all was the walled garden, which brothers Douglas and Kenneth McDowall, last of the direct line, converted into a home for tender and sub-tropical plants which normally cannot be grown outside in Britain. Here the brothers pioneered the use of peat terrace walls in peat gardens. This feature can be seen at Logan today on the site of the brothers' historic innovation. Since 1969 the walled garden, together with a small area outside it, has been an outstation of the Royal Botanic Garden in Edinburgh.

Ardwell's origins as an estate village are obvious in this view looking north towards Sandhead and Stranraer. The last cottage on the right became a gospel hall while the field beyond was in the Second World War the site of a small prisoner of war camp for Italian POW's working on local farms. Despite its placid appearance, the clachan was in past times the venue for a traditional event, the Leek Fair, which was notorious for alcohol-fuelled disorder. Even more extreme violence in the vicinity is indicated by the presence of the Murder Stone in the garden of an Ardwell House lodge just out of the top of the photo. It records the denouement of the rivalry between two local lairds' sons for the hand (and lands) of the heiress of nearby Portencorkrie now Barncorkrie. Involved were abduction, headlong but vain pursuit, ambush, and the death of young Macdouall of Logan at the hands of the followers of his rival, Gordon of Clanyard.

In Ardwell's commercial quarter at the south end of the village the two-storey building has been at various times co-operative store, privately owned general store with tailoring and bootmaking facilities, and, as here, private house. The building on the right with the porch started life as a coaching inn, became a hotel, and then took on the role of a shop from its neighbour. What the driver and passengers of the original horse-drawn coach would have made of the impressive range of early twentieth century wheeled transport on display is an interesting speculation. Clearly Ardwell was not a place for rapid change: the Henry and then the McCamon families owned the general store for a combined total of 100 years.

As we saw in the case of Ardwell, two miles to the east, Wigtownsire villages, like those elsewhere, were till at least the mid-twentieth century much more self-sufficient than is the case today. Thus in 1918 Clachanmore at its crossroads had a public school (on the left beside the wood), a joiner's shop (out of sight beyond the single-storey, white, school annexe and at right angles to it), a general store (the first building in the row beyond the crossroads) and a smithy out of sight on the right. Smithy and joiner's shop may be out of sight but they were the most important buildings in the village. Until the Second World War motive power on farms was provided by Clydesdale horses of the kind ploughing in the foreground while the carts they pulled were, of course, wooden. The blacksmith's and joiner's skills were essential to keep the rural economy functioning. Old habits die hard: the general store closed only in 1981.

Wigtownshire has a tradition of idiosyncratic cave dwellers taking up residence on its shores. Arguably it goes back to the days of Alexander Bain, better known by the local version of his name, Sawney Bean, and even better known for his carnivorous habits. Will Purves, who lived in Sheeprink Co' on the North Channel coast near Clachanmore had, as far as is known, no dietary peculiarities. A former circus strongman from London, he was not a hermit but enjoyed spending his evenings in the local (male only) social club, the Clachanmore smithy.

Smithies in Wigtownshire usually performed this function, where attenders could enjoy plenty of company and witness not only the blacksmith's metalworking skills but also his considerable medical talents. Thus in addition to their social function, country smithies were often the local minor accident and ailment unit. But Will was not an ideal member of the social club. Angered on one occasion by a remark, he left, taking the anvil with him and depositing it at the crossroads a quarter of a mile away.

The east side of Luce Bay from New England Bay to Sandhead is dotted with the remains, some insubstantial, of small-scale, mainly water-powered industries. One such is Dye Mill, a mile north of Ardwell, which performed not only the function stated by the name but also that of a waulk mill, a reminder of the importance of the linen industry in Stoneykirk Parish. Motive power came from the waters of the modest-sized Alwhibbie Burn, which flows close to the gable nearer the camera. It has been plausibly suggested that for its dye mill role the enterprise may have used mosses, lichens, and seaweeds from the shore close by. The part of the building with the lower roof was the mill and the part further from the camera the miller's house. Water was an imperfect source of motive power in this area of low rainfall and another solution was occasionally attempted. This industrial strip is bookended by two windmills, Logan Windmill south of Ardwell village and Culgroat Windmill north of Sandhead.

The meal (corn) mill like this one at Ardwell was a key element in the estate economy. Tenants were thirled to the mill: they were required to have all their corn ground there and the requirement was strictly enforced. As payment the tenant had to give the miller a stated fraction of the ground corn, known as multures. The multures received by the miller determined the rent he paid the laird for the mill, hence the strict enforcement of the system. Eventually multures were converted into money payments and as such lasted into the twentieth century. Ardwell was a large mill with four sets of stones, one for beans, for which tenants also would be thirled. The mill was in use in 1967 but part of it has now been demolished, including the chimney. The latter is something of a puzzle as the machinery was never steam-powered. It may have been connected with the large kiln which formed part of the complex.

A big mill like Ardwell required a substantial and reliable source of water and this was provided in the usual way by a dam, mill pond, and lade. The generous-sized mill pond was supplied by the Cairnweil Burn and situated alongside the A716 at Doctor's Corner opposite the road to Kirkmadrine. The site today is covered by scrub and reeds. In anticipation of our contemporary concerns the water was recycled after use at the meal mill, being used to power a small mill connected with the flax industry and situated close to the shore at the bottom of the glen. Today only traces of this small relative are left. Our picture appears to show the lade in disrepair after water power had been replaced by electricity following an interesting period when, in another anticipation of our times, water power had been used to drive a turbine. In some rural Wigtownshire enterprises the age of steam never arrived.

Of modest size and inconspicuous location, Kirkmadrine Church on its hillock overlooking Luce Bay is nevertheless the second oldest Christian site in Scotland. Its three fifth-century memorial stones to three high-ranking churchmen are, as Christian monuments, exceeded in antiquity only by one at Whithorn across the bay. The discovery of the stones utilised as gate posts close by is a remarkable one. Their presence in the area indicates the existence in the fifth century of an important religious establishment here but what it was, why it was built in this remote spot, and its relationship to the monastery at Whithorn, Scotland's first Christian foundation, are subjects of perennial discussion. Kirkmadrine's later story is more certain. The medieval church on this site served the parish of Toskarton until the latter ceased to exist in 1618 on its amalgamation with Stoneykirk. The present mausoleum-chapel was erected by the McTaggart Stewarts of Ardwell in the late nineteenth century and houses the fifth-century stones in a glassed-in porch.

The whitewashed cottages that comprised most of Sandhead's main street were traditionally the homes of farm workers and fishermen and their families: a nineteenth century writer commented that the village had "a sort of amphibious aspect". The little building in the left foreground with the diminutive spire and ecclesiastical-looking gable window is in fact the village school in use from 1875 until 1941, when a new school was opened on the higher ground behind at Stairmount. Although Sandhead has always been the largest settlement in the parish, the village did not become the kirkton, the location of the parish church, until 1963. The original kirkton in this area was the lost village of Toskarton, which stood at or close to where the road to Kirkmadrine church turns off the Doctor's Corner to Clachanmore Road. The village, which owed its existence to the church, was abandoned sometime after the latter lost its parish church status in 1618. So thorough was the process that today it is hard to see any traces of Toskarton's existence.

The north end of Sandhead is also dominated by whitewashed cottages, now all vanished, but the row of buildings on the right included a farm, a common feature of Wigtownshire villages, and a smithy, an indispensable component of the rural scene. On the skyline behind the telegraph pole is a mound like an upturned pudding bowl, indicating the location of a twelfth century wooden castle or motte The fact that the village street is lined up on the motte suggests it is contemporary with the latter and so hundreds of years older than is generally assumed. Supporting evidence for the village's antiquity comes from its name, which is entirely English unlike most place names in the area. This suggests that Sandhead may have been founded, occupied, and named by Anglo-Saxon retainers of the Anglo-Norman lord who had built the castle. In the background on the left is Sandhead Creamery, one of nine creameries operating in Wigtownshire in 1955. Today that number is reduced to one.

The history of Sandhead Creamery is typical of several small creameries in Wigtownshire. Founded as a farmers' co-operative, it was taken over by the Scottish Milk Marketing Board when that body was formed in 1933. Because of its distance from centres of population and lack of a rail link, it concentrated on the production of cheese. The whey which was a by-product fed the pigs in the creamery's piggery down on the shore until its closure in 1944. The creamery itself was closed in the 1960s but somewhat unusually reopened in 1972 under the ownership of J. and M. Bell, who operated a dairy nearby from Sandmill Farm with an extensive milk round. They used the creamery to pasteurise their milk, including Jersey milk. After its final closure in 1991 the building was converted into flats. Sandhead could claim two major achievements: in 1954 in conjunction with the Kraft firm it became the first SMMB creamery to manufacture cheese in 40lb blocks instead of traditional cylindrical cheese and in the same period it won the world championship for Stilton cheese.

The Wigtownshire landscape is studded with mottes: Sandhead's version, known as Balgreggan Motte after the local estate, has counterparts in Ardwell and Drummore villages to the south with Terally and Clanyard Mottes also in the immediate neighbourhood. Most are the consequence of the policy followed by King David of Scotland in the twelfth century to curb his restless Galloway subjects. The limited success of the strategy is attested by Balgreggan Motte. Erosion on the inland side has revealed lumps of burned wood, clear evidence that the wooden structure on its earthen mound had been destroyed by fire during one of the intermittent uprisings against non-indigenous rule in the late twelfth and early thirteenth centuries. Balgreggan was involved in a later conflict. In the Second World War the local branch of the Royal Observer Corps had an observation post there to the detriment of the surviving archaeology.

The number plate of the vehicle in the foreground fixes the time of this picture in the early to mid-twentieth century, with the Commercial Hotel not yet metamorphosed into the Tigh-na-Mara. The deceptive spire of the school is visible in the right background but not so the Volunteers' drill hall which stood just beyond it and later became the village hall. The rifle range on the shore north of the village was presumably connected with the local Volunteers detachment. The building on the left partly obscured by the trees was the carpet bowling hall. The stretch of road rising up the raised beach in the background is known as the Battery, perhaps because of the coast protection buttresses on the shore at the foot of the steep slope. Just visible in the left background is the place where the 5-mile sandy beach along the head of the bay gives way to stones and shingle, giving the village its name.

For long the South Rhinns Peninsula depended almost entirely on sea transport, which utilised not only regular harbours but also the sandy or shingle beaches particularly on the east side where a small coasting vessel could run ashore at high tide. It then unloaded its coal or lime or loaded agricultural produce at low tide and departed on the next high tide. The practice was still in use in the late 1940s. With its enormous sandy beach Sandhead was an ideal informal landing place. Thus in the background a line of farm carts and horses waits patiently to load or unload the cargo. The era of the primacy of sea transport was ended by the arrival of the internal combustion engine and this brought a change of role for the beach, anticipated by the group in the foreground. The spread of car ownership and bus transport made possible trips to the seaside and Sandhead became very popular with residents from nearby Stranraer and visitors from further afield

Until recent housing developments Stoneykirk had the unusual shape of an inverted A with its apex to the south. The cause for this is the Stoneykirk bypass, surely one of the first of its kind. The straggle of houses running across the picture in the background behind the church marks the line of the old Stranraer to Drummore road. It meanders through the village negotiating en route an awkward bridge across a burn. and forms the right leg of the A. This obstacle course was eliminated for through traffic by 1875, with the formation of a bypass, which forms the left leg of the A. A minor road formed the crosspiece of the A and ribbon development on it and the new bypass gave the village its shape. The houses on the new road can be seen in the foreground. The 1000-capacity parish church, built in 1827, seems inappropriately large for the small clachan yet in 1839 the minister declared it too small "when the inhabitants are disposed to attend".

Stoneykirk School, closed over sixty years ago and now converted to a house, stood on the crosspiece of the village's idiosyncratic, inverted-A, street plan. In 1839 the predecessors of those pupils enjoyed a nutritious educational diet with the traditional three R's supplemented by Latin, Greek, French, and book-keeping, the last four subjects requiring an extra five shillings a quarter in school fees. In this pre-state school era the fees were an important element in the master's salary. In Stoneykirk the latter amounted to an annual £25.13.3, paid as usual (often reluctantly) by the heritors, the landed proprietors of the parish. The dominie's salary was supplemented by approximately £10 in fees per year. The later incumbent, Mr. Robertson, like his school, has not been admitted to the photograph although he was Stoneykirk schoolmaster for 39 years.

Lochans village and mill form an inconspicuous background to a display of some of the famous herd of Shorthorn cattle belonging to the Marshall dynasty of Bridgebank between Lochans and Stoneykirk. The herd is more readily associated with another Marshall farm, Cruggleton near Garlieston. Father Matthew (Mattha) and son Albert James (Bertie) traded in high quality animals and pioneered the export of Shorthorns to Argentina. In 1918 the Marshalls paid the then record price for a Shorthorn bull of 3,700 guineas. The dispersal sale of the herd at Cruggleton in 1952 was a major event in Scottish farming. However Mattha had made the Marshall name internationally known long before then with another breed, Clydesdale horses. Rather unfairly described in an official 1890 document as a "horse dealer", from his Bridgebank base he bought and sold Clydesdales at the top end of the market as well as breeding and exhibiting them. By 1895 he was winning championships at national shows and went on to export Clydesdales to the USA, Canada, Russia, and South Africa.

The contrasting, patterned, brick surrounds of the doors and windows of Lochans Post Office are a feature found also in Drummore's Mill Street. According to an 1875 guide the village possessed several other facilities: the obligatory smithy and joiner's workshop together with "a respectable...grocery store and a large school". What the village did not possess however was a rail link and this in spite of the fact that the Stranraer-Portpatrick section of the line to Castle Douglas and Dumfries ran less than half a mile to the north and Lochans was the only settlement on this section. The Lochans situation illustrates a bone of contention between the railway company

and local communities across Galloway. For the company the primary aim was to cater for through passengers travelling by ferry to and from Northern Ireland while local people thought the priority should be to serve the local area. The position of stations, timetables, and the line of the railway itself all reflected the company philosophy.

The story of Portpatrick is largely the story of its harbour, for 5,000 years the Scottish terminal of the short sea route between Great Britain and Ireland. However the story suggested by the present harbour is totally deceptive. The only harbour-like area is the inner basin in the left foreground. But by the time it was constructed in 1861-64 Portpatrick's glory days were over for the mail service and the regular ferry service had left. For most of the previous millennia the landing place had in fact been the small arc of beach in the right-hand middle ground. It could take only small, flat-bottomed boats; when the era of larger vessels dawned, they had to lie outside the bay and transfer their cargoes to small craft. Because of Portpatrick's strategic importance in communications with often troublesome Ireland the government tried to improve facilities in 1770 by bringing in famous civil engineer John Smeaton. He built breakwaters and a pier beside the beach but the sea treated his efforts with contempt.

The inner basin may lie snugly under the hotel but Portpatrick's major problem was at the other end of the harbour. The narrow, rocky entrance in the left middleground made entering and leaving in a westerly wind of any strength a considerable hazard. Deception seems to be a feature of Portpatrick for the railway line in the right foreground appears to be about to attempt to cross the North Channel to Ireland but in prosaic fact its destination is Stranraer, the rails reaching the coast south of the village before turning north and then north-east to run inland to the terminus. The inhospitable nature of Wigtownshire's North Channel coast, The Back Shore, and consequent difficulty of finding good harbours is well illustrated.

In 1821, with John Smeaton's harbour largely ruined and the need for improved communication with Ireland as great as ever, the government tried again at Portpatrick, commissioning famous Scottish civil engineer John Rennie to design and build an improved harbour. Rennie's plan was boldly ambitious: to eliminate the entrance problem by building a new harbour on the seaward side of it. This involved constructing two enormous piers out into the North Channel and linking them at the landward end by a curving breakwater cum promenade, the whole forming a huge letter U with its arms converging towards the entrance. A substantial part of the landward section of the south pier survives but the pile of rubble at its base tells an ominous story. The south pier was completed but then badly damaged by a gale and funds had to be diverted from the north pier to repair it, a situation which kept recurring. The pillar on the left of the pier wall is all that remained of Smeaton's pier.

Starved of funds the north pier, at a planned 800' compared to its neighbour's 500', was never completed. After 28 weary years, during much of which time the village was a vast industrial site, patience and money ran out. The government transferred the mail service to Greenock and with it went the ferry service. Portpatrick's glory days were over. The remains of the outer and inner walls of the north pier, built of Welsh limestone and stone from Dunbartonshire are visible in the right foreground. The space between was filled with stone (hearting) from the vast quarry at the south end of the village. The depredations of the sea mean that very little of the north pier is to be seen today apart from piles of large dressed stones that have been contemptuously hurled around by the waves.

The railway age saw the government's last attempt to improve Portpatrick Harbour with the construction from 1861 till 1864 of the inner basin. It contributed little to the story of the village's involvement with the short sea route, playing host only to a few short-lived attempts by private companies to run a regular ferry service together with a number of excursions in both directions. It found a more useful role as a landing facility for the catches of local and visiting fishing boats but only after Portpatrick's best years as a fishing port were over. Herring fishing was at its peak from 1813 till 1821 with the local fleet of around twenty boats augmented by another hundred visiting vessels during the two-month season from early June. After withdrawal of government grant put paid to the herring fishing, cod fishing became popular on a modest scale with ten local boats and thirty fishermen involved. Specimens like these could weigh up to 40 pounds. By 1965 it was reported that very little fishing was done by local men although visiting boats still used the basin.

Hand-in-hand with the attempts to improve Portpatrick Harbour went the upgrading of land communications from Carlisle to Portpatrick to speed the passage of troops to fractious Ireland. From 1763 till 1765 soldier labour was used to build a military road between those two places. It consisted largely of a major reconstruction of existing or old roads with some realignment. On the most westerly section the Old Military Road keeps companionably close to the A75 from Newton Stewart to Stranraer but then abandons it from there to Portpatrick only for the two to be reunited and become one in Portpatick Main Street 200 yards from the harbour. The military road swoops down the brae past the school and the union is effected at the old church just beyond the parked cars on the right. Returning residents of Ireland would be slightly confused to discover the large building on the right is The Downshire Arms Hotel.

The inner basin in the right middleground symbolises Portpatrick's past as a ferry port while the hotel on the cliff behind is a signpost to its future. Deprived of the umbilical cord of the short sea route to Ireland, the village reinvented itself as a holiday resort. A crucial role in the transformation was played by the laird of Dunskey, Charles Orr Ewing. In 1905 he built the Portpatrick Hotel, capable of accommodating more than 100 guests and "furnished regardless of expense and lighted throughout by electricity"; the generating system which lit the hotel also lit the village streets, making Portpatrick the first village in Wigtownshire to enjoy that distinction. Despite the handsome motor car (the first in Portpatrick) centre stage, it was another form of transport which at first played the major part in conveying visitors to the fledgling resort.

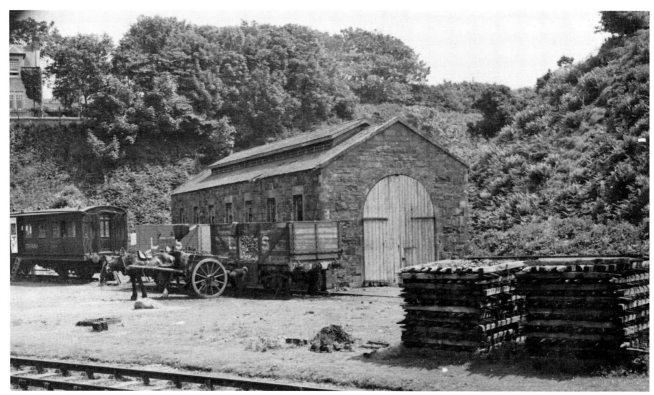

As the name indicates, The Portpatrick Railway Company was established to link the national rail network with the short sea route to Ireland at that village. The railway duly reached "The Port" in 1862 with a branch line from the station to the quayside of the new basin. However, the latter was not ready for use until 1864, by which time a daily steamer service had been running from Stranraer to Larne for two years. Portpatrick had literally and finally missed the boat. But the new railway had an important role to play in the village's reincarnation as a holiday resort. It was until the 1930s the principal form of transport for arriving and departing visitors. Thus in a 1915 guide The Downshire Arms announces that "Boots meets all Trains" while two firms offer to convey luggage to and from the station. Day excursions not only from Stranraer but also Glasgow and Paisley were very popular in the 1920s. The station was at the east end of the village.

Portpatrick soon acquired all the necessary trappings of a seaside resort. In 1915 eleven boarding houses ("guest houses" in modern parlance) were advertising their attractions. Back in 1901 A. Campbell's Branch Order Office for Portpatrick Hotel Stables had advertised itself in this category, offering two sitting (rooms) and five bedrooms with or without board but "with good attendance". Mr Campbell also offered posting in open or closed carriages. It seems that at a later date he entered a merger with Portpatrick Hotel, becoming manager of the establishment he formerly owned. The appearance of the building in Harbour Place just 100 yards from the sea suggests it still retained its dual function.

DUNSKEY GLEN

Portpatrick's advocates eloquently extolled the natural attractions of the village for holidaymakers. High among those was Dunskey Glen on the estate of that name just north of Portpatrick. "One of the most picturesque glens in Galloway", it twists from Port Kale on the shore up the narrow valley of the Dunskey Burn through a diversity of flowers, shrubs, and trees (with a waterfall thrown in for good measure) to a rendezvous with the public road. At Port Kale the submarine cable, originally telegraph, later telephone, and now obsolete, came ashore. Dunskey, from the Gaelic, may mean "The shielded fort", a reference to the castle on the south side of Portpatrick, former residence of the local lairds.

The lady on the left walking up Braefield Road has been availing herself of another of Portpatrick's assets, the pure sea water, ideal, we are assured, for bathing. With its chalybeate spring the village tended to market itself as a spa, the bracing air also being stressed. However, the claim in a 1901 guidebook that this is a place "where 'The Sick Man' is unknown" seems to stray perilously close to the bounds of credibility. Behind the right shoulder of the bathing queen can be glimpsed one buttress of the bridge which carried the railway branch line from the station to the quayside. The line was barely used and soon closed, with the later removal of the bridge platform. In the right middleground stands St. Ninian's Scottish Episcopal church, built in 1937, perhaps an unexpected sight in such a small community.

29

Portpatrick did not rely solely on natural assets to succeed as a holiday resort. Charles Orr Ewing of Dunskey, whose electricity supply and fine hotel have already been cited, made another major contribution by providing an eighteen-hole golf course, opened in 1903. The postponement of the opening from April till June because of bad weather proved not to be an ill omen for the club flourished. A separate ladies' clubhouse was added in 1904 while in 1914 the acquisition of more ground along the cliff top allowed the creation of a second, nine-hole course to complement the original one. The provision of ladies' facilities, albeit segregated, only a year after the course opened indicates that in terms of membership this was a club ahead of its time. Yet in 1952 it still imposed a geographical restriction, for according to the official handbook only permanent residents of the Rhinns could be ordinary members.

Situated close to the busy North Channel shipping lanes on a stretch of coast resembling a gigantic mantrap, Portpatrick was an obvious choice for a lifeboat station and one was established in 1877, being still operational today. This boat is the *Jeanie Spiers*, which served here from 1937 till 1961. Of her 66 launches the most famous was her participation in the ill-starred search for the crippled Stranraer-Larne ferry *Princess Victoria*, which sank with the loss of 133 lives in a January gale in 1953. The lifeboat was powered by two engines unlike her predecessor *Civil Service No. 3* (1900-1922), pictured on Page 26, which relied on twelve double-banked oars and a small sail. *No. 3* was usually kept in the boathouse (now the lifeboat shop) to be launched and retrieved at low tide by means of a crane. At high tide she was run on rails to the edge of the inner basin and propelled into the water with the assistance of a roller.

Like their counterparts at Port Logan and Drummore the Portpatrick coast guard unit included in their ranks a rocket crew, demonstrating their skills here. The apparatus was used to rescue the crews of ships wrecked close to the shore. The rocket carried a line out to the distressed vessel, initiating the setting up a breeches buoy, which conveyed the crew to safety by means of an early but deadly serious form of zipwire. Its effectiveness was demonstrated in 1898 when the barque *Firth of Cromarty* ran on to rocks less than a mile south of Corsewall Lighthouse. The Portpatrick rocket brigade rescued fourteen men from the wrecked ship. They also earned a walk-on part in Wigtownshire's real-life version of the book and film *Whisky Galore* for among the ship's mixed cargo was a large consignment of bottled whisky, much of which evaded the recovery efforts of H.M. Customs and Excise.

Built in 1900, Killantringan lighthouse was one of a chain of four attempting to tame the hostility of The Rhinns' North Channel coast. Two miles north of Portpatrick, it replaced a long succession of lighthouses in that village. Killantringan reached the national headlines in February, 1982, when the Cypriot vessel *Craigantlet* outward bound from Belfast Lough with a mixed cargo ran onto rocks below the lighthouse in seemingly innocuous weather. As the ship began to break up in subsequent heavy seas, it emerged she was carrying drums of chemical waste and a major operation was undertaken to prevent calamitous pollution. This postcard was written in April, 1936, by the wife of a newly arrived keeper at Killantringan, who adds a human touch to the lighthouse's story. She thinks the couple's new station looks "very nice" and they are liking it despite the cold and rain. The Killantringan light is now dark as a result of advances in marine navigational equipment.

Around 1750 Dinvin Mill on the outskirts of Portpatrick acquired a new tenant, a well known family who had been practising their trade in Wigtownshire since at least the seventeenth century. Prior to Dinvin the Hannays had been at Barhoise Mill near Kirkcowan. When they moved, they put a tree trunk through the axle hole of each millstone and rolled the stones from Kirkcowan to Portpatrick by way of the challenging gradients of the Old Port Road. The Hannays were not just skilled millers for at a later date one of them invented a machine for more efficient grinding of the oats. It was highly successful, in 1912 earning its inventor a princely £1000 in royalties. Arguably the mill is a microcosm

of the development of the village. It began life in the service industry then part of it became a hotel, contributing to tourism. Now it has been converted into a house, reflecting the dramatic growth of private housing on Portpatrick's margins.

Enoch Farm, two hundred yards north of the junction of the Old Port Road with the A77 a mile outside Portpatrick, has as close neighbours two reminders of the village's importance as a link with Ireland. Just behind the farm buildings is a stretch of the Old Military Road, constructed from 1763 to 1765 to accelerate military deployment to Ireland. The troops building this section, mainly Royal Scots Fusiliers, worked from June till October and daily from 3 a.m. until midday. On the hill above stands a BT microwave radio mast, used until recent times by various organisations for a variety of purposes. Through it the Independent Television Authority linked Ulster Television with the rest of the TV network; it also carried BT telephone traffic. Advances in telecommunications have made the mast redundant. The name Enoch suggests another possible type of activity here for its Gaelic meaning is "market". Did traders crossing from Ireland set up stall just out of reach of Portpatrick bureaucracy to lighten their loads and weigh down their pockets?

An 1875 writer's description of cottages at the clachan of Foulford on the south-west edge of Stranraer seems equally applicable to this solitary example: "They are very literally 'auld clay biggins'. Their walls are of clay, mixed with a little chopped straw and stones while the roofs and chimneys are of straw." The result may be picturesque but was uncomfortable to live in. For a good part of the twentieth century Wigtownshire was notorious for the poor quality of its rural housing. Indeed at the 1939 Church of Scotland General Assembly in Edinburgh the question of Wigtownshire' poor rural housing conditions was raised by a Rhinns minister. At the same time a Stranraer presbytery committee recorded that in the majority of rural houses they had visited no sanitation was provided and people had to walk some hundred yards for water. And a 1955 report stated that more than one third (1561) of houses in the landward area were unfit for habitation with 800 of them beyond repair.

Running down the side of Meikle's Hotel ("Replete with every convenience for Private Families, Tourists, and Commercial Gentlemen") South Strand Street is the southern section of the oldest street in Stranraer. Beneath it, in a culvert, runs the feature which gave Stranraer its existence, the Town Burn. The first houses in the settlement stood on its banks, those on the east side expanding into the clachan of Chapel (or Clachan of St. John) and those on the west into the village of Stranraer, the two eventually merging to form the nucleus of the fledgling burgh. In 1683 the remains of an ancient boat were dug up at the far end of the street on its left-hand side. Sadly nothing of it has survived. In the 1950s the street played host to a very different form of transport when the one-storey former stables, by then converted into a garage, were used as a checkpoint for cars departing from Glasgow in the famous Monte Carlo rally.

In 1952 George Street bears no great signs of antiquity but in fact along with its eastern extension Charlotte Street it is the second oldest thoroughfare in Stranraer. Those two streets stand on the line of Cross Street, which as its name implies traversed the Town Burn. As late as the seventeenth century the essential town plan of Stranraer consisted of the two original streets plus three vennels, the modern King, Queen, and Princes Streets, running down from the western part of Cross Street to the shore, which was on the line of the present Fisher Street. The sinuous nature of George Street may be the result of spasmodic, random development or an attempt to filter out some of the notorious prevailing westerly winds. The photograph is taken from the same spot as the previous one but the photographer is looking west instead of south.

The view north down Castle Street in the former clachan of Chapel probably encompasses the site of the elusive source of the settlement's name for the chapel stood on the east side of the burn close to the later castle. Built in 1484 by a lady member of the powerful Adair family, it was tactfully dedicated to St. John for the land had belonged to the Knights of the Order of St. John of Jerusalem. The link with St. John is perpetuated in the name of a nearby street. Foundation work some years ago on the corner of Castle Street and Charlotte Street (on the right) failed to uncover any traces of an earlier building. The most promising site appears to be the corner of North Strand Street and Charlotte Street. One of the town's best known hotels, The King's Arms, now vanished without trace,. stood at the north end of Castle Street on the right.

Hugged companionably at this time by its neighbours, the Castle of St. John is Stranraer's oldest extant building. It was built around 1520 by the powerful Adair family of Kinhilt. The tradition that the stones for it were conveyed hand-to-hand by a line of men stretching from the Adair seat outside Lochans to Stranraer should perhaps be treated with a degree of caution. Among later residents was Graham of Claverhouse, scourge of the Covenanters, who made it his temporary home in 1677 while seeking to cleanse the area of his arch-foes. Over the years the castle has much altered in both appearance and function. Particularly unsuccessful was the use from 1820 until 1840 of the upper two floors as a prison, a period characterised by drunken jailers, doors left unlocked, and, inevitably, disappearing prisoners.

Known locally as "The Cross", the area at the junction of George Street and Church Street was the civic heart of old Stranraer for here were located the structures that proclaimed the town's burgh status (baronial in 1596, royal in 1617). Most important was the tolbooth, on the right, with its distinctive clock tower, belfry, and spire. Built in 1776, it replaced a predecessor located in the middle of the street and was a one-stop shop, performing a range of civic functions. Close to the tolbooth stood the mercat cross, indicating the site for fairs and markets and the place where important public announcements were made. Its exact location is unknown, but it seems likely that it stood where in this view the wrought-iron fountain commemorating the 60th anniversary of Queen Victoria's accession stands. Similarly the exact location of the public weighbeam, the tron, is not known but it stood first in the centre of the street and then at the head of Queen Street (the Mid Vennel) .

Running directly south from The Cross, Lewis Street was originally known as Stoneykirk Lane but metamorphosed into its present designation to commemorate a local landowner. A more suitable name might be Street of Spires or to be strictly accurate Rooftop Appendages. First up, on the extreme left is the bell tower of the former Free Church of Scotland, now Lewis Street Gospel Hall. Beyond the trees on the left looms the impressive bulk of the New Town Hall and Courthouse, "perhaps the finest public building in Galloway". Immediately beyond is the pointed spire of the West United Presbyterian Church, latterly St. Ninian's Church of Scotland,

in "endearingly lumpy Gothic" style, to quote a recent architectural guide. Most important of all, historically speaking, is the spire immediately above the horse and cart, of the former parish church, built in 1841 and the latest in a series on or close to the same site going back to the original parish church, erected in 1649 to fulfil a condition of elevation to royal burgh status.

SEA BANK ROAD, STRANRAER.

The house on the left is the western extremity of Clayhole, one of the five clachans which coalesced into modern Stranraer, not always with the residents' approval: in the 1870s dwellers in Clayhole and Hillhead objected to paying Stranraer rates on the grounds they were not part of that entity. Admittedly this may be an early example of attempted tax avoidance rather than an expression of separate identity. Clayhole for some reason is part of local popular culture and widely used in an uncomplimentary sense to describe the place of origin of natives of Stranraer. The gates in the right foreground lead to Seabank House, the former residence of a famous name in local maritime history, Captain George Campbell. Master of the first steamer to provide a daily service between Stranraer and Northern Ireland, he went on to give 36 years of service to the its route and for thousands of travellers was personification.

Stranraer is not a natural harbour; the position before 1820 is described in a nineteenth century guidebook: "Large vessels anchored in the roadstead; those of lighter draught came in with the flood tide and being left high and dry discharged their cargoes into carts. Passengers by the steamer *Dumbarton Castle* were landed in small boats and on the backs of men who waded in the water." This unsatisfactory state of affairs was remedied in that year by the construction of a pier, the West Pier, (middleground) subsequently extended. The Railway Pier (background) was built in 1861 to provide a pierhead connection between the newly arrived railway and the Irish ferry. Built by the council and leased to the railway company, it proved so unfit for purpose that the railway authorities successfully petitioned parliament to be allowed to take over ownership and effect the necessary improvements. To the right of the West Pier, the Breastwork, site of manure stores and horse fairs, stands on reclaimed land.

The £3,800 cost of the West Pier caused the council severe financial difficulties for many ships refused to pay the harbour dues and a legal appeal found in their favour. Putting a chain across the entrance to bar entry to non-payers proved only partly successful for ships simply beached gratis in Clayhole Bay in the middleground to the left of the lampost on the quay. The Stranraer-registered boat tied up alongside the pier indicates an improvement in the situation since 1764, when the port possessed only two small vessels. Clayhole Bay is appropriately named for much of the material for building Stranraer's early houses was extracted from here.

The notice "Steamers" just behind the clock shows how easy the transfer from train to ship was at the station on the Railway Pier, for an exit beside the uniformed official led to the steamer gangplank just a few yards away. In 1912 at the height of the suffragette movement this platform was the scene of an incident involving no less than Winston Churchill. Crossing from ferry to train on his return from a political meeting in Belfast, he was hit in the face by a small flag wielded by a London-based lady of the suffragette persuasion. The First Sea Lord, as he then was, made political capital from the incident by interceding to prevent the lady being physically abused by the incensed (male) crowd before making an impromptu speech from his compartment window prior to the London train's departure.

The *Princess Victoria* which joined the Stranraer-Larne service in 1890 was the first of four vessels to bear that name, the fourth and surely last being the ill-starred 1947 version. The 1890 paddle steamer set new standards for her time with electric light and seven watertight bulkheads, which unlike the later *Titanic*, were carried up to main deck level. Accommodation for 700 cattle is a reminder that some livestock still used the short sea route. On her first day on the run the *Victoria* ran into and severely damaged a schooner, fortunately without fatalities. In 1892 the steamer hove to off Corsewall Point with a damaged paddle, sending out distress signals, A passing ship offered to tow her into Stranraer for £500 but the *Victoria*'s captain held out for £250. With negotiations at a stalemate the *Victoria*'s sister ferry arrived and took her in tow to the chagrin of the would-be salver.

When she entered service in 1904 the *Princess Maud* was the first turbine steamer on any Irish Sea service. Perhaps unusually for the time attempts were made to cater adequately for all classes: while there were four staterooms for first class passengers, in another contrast with the ill-starred *Titanic* steerage passengers were well provided for, their amenities including a ladies' lounge. However the *Maud*'s career was blighted by controversy. Proceeding up Loch Ryan on a foggy morning in 1909 she ran into the cargo ship *Pirate* inconsiderately anchored in the shipping channel. Although the cargo ship sank in ten minutes, no casualties were incurred, even a passenger's cat being saved. However, the ferry company dismissed the *Maud*'s master, presumably "pour encourager les autres".

The 1890s saw a big increase nationally in the steamer excursion trade, an early response to the modern challenge of keeping expensive technology as fully used as possible. Stranraer-based ferries used the Railway Pier, a frequent destination being the Ayrshire coast and Ailsa Craig. However a hiccup occurred in 1897 when the *Princess May*, fortunately with less than 200 passengers, broke a paddle wheel off the latter island and limped home eighteen hours late. Besides the local company's offerings shipping agent George Watson enterprisingly chartered steamers from outside companies, using the West Pier. For example, in August, 1895, he hired the Glasgow and South-Western steamer *Glen Rosa* for an excursion to Rothesay. Other Watson excursion destinations included Campbeltown, Tarbert, Dunoon, and Arrochar, the vessel sometimes being the G&SWR *Juno*. The departure point, and the type and paint scheme of the ship suggest this may be one of Mr Watson's initiatives.

The sight of the *Caledonian Princess* berthed at the Railway Pier in December, 1961, was a huge relief to the local community. Since the loss of *Princess Victoria* in January, 1953, temporary arrangements had been used to cover the gap. Failure to produce a permanent replacement led to growing anxiety that the British Transport Commission intended to close down the route, an anxiety not lessened by that body's contradictory statements on the subject. Intensive lobbying was necessary before the new ship eventually sailed up the loch. The *Caledonian Princess* was a Janus-like vessel in that she looked both backwards and forwards. Thoroughly traditional features of her design included ample sleeping accommodation for passengers wishing to avoid an early rise to catch the 7.00 sailing and the provision of pens for cattle and sheep below the car deck. On the other hand the giving over of the entire main deck to motor vehicles and the plethora of lounges, bar, cafes, and restaurants anticipated features of her successors.

The sea provided Stranraer with another source of employment besides the ferry service, and the fishing industry was not always conducted on the modest scale seen here. The 1791 *Statistical Account* records that formerly the herring fishery in Loch Ryan had been very important with boats coming from all quarters to participate, sometimes 300 at a time, creating employment and wealth. But it had now much declined, yielding only scanty catches sufficient for local needs. The 1839 *Account* records that the shoals of herring had deserted the loch for many years and that local fishermen were not interested in catching the abundance of other varieties available presumably because no market existed for them. The 1965 *Account* reports further decline with very few fishermen left. The 1839 complaint that local fishermen were interested only in herring echoes recent comments by two visiting celebrity chefs, Nick Nairn and Paul Rankin, who lamented that the Scottish public seemed uninterested in adding to their limited dietary fish preferences from the rich offerings round our shores.

Broadstone Road with its eye-catching variety of domestic architecture has changed little since 1967 but the skyline beyond with its evidence of Stranraer's industries has altered dramatically. Like other Scottish towns of similar size and location the burgh's industrial sector mainly consisted of small enterprises processing the products of local agriculture. Thus left of centre the chimney with accompanying building on its right is the Wigtownshire Creamery, established by local farmers and businessmen in 1884, and taken over in 1916 by the Scottish Co-operative Wholesale Society. While the creamery has totally disappeared, the small jars, originally filled with cream ("a rare table delicacy"), which formed one of its main lines, are to be found on the shelves of many a collectables shop. To the right of the creamery the square tower signals the site of Sheuchan Mill, final destination after a leisurely circuit of The Rhinns of the well known Hannay family of millers. The now vanished mill, like the creamery, is testimony to the modern concentration of industry into large, centrally situated units.

Stranraer is the largest town west of Dumfries and the retail centre for a large area. Consequently some of its shops have echoes of their urban counterparts. The name of The Glasgow House seems to suggest affinities with city emporia and the firm's adverts in the local paper encouraged that idea. Potential customers were promised "keen-cut prices that defy competition" and at the same time the latest in haute couture: "showrooms a veritable Style Paradise…millinery collection of Paris and London creations." Whether competitors Caldow's Bargain Stores and McDowall's Central Warehouse were in fact defied is not recorded but the fact that this was "A cash…warehouse" would hardly encourage today's seekers after retail therapy. The Glasgow House has gone from the town but the frontage, perhaps reflecting the firm's aspirations, still stands in George Street.

The ferry service to Ireland brought a steady income to Stranraer's hotels and guest houses. Prominent among the former was The King's Arms in Castle Street, where in 1901 proprietor W. MacRobert offered an establishment "replete with every convenience", including, puzzlingly, "A large show room". Certainly the entrance hall was not bare of ornament. This very hall featured in the 1930 best-selling whodunnit *Sir John Magill's Last Journey* by Freeman Wills Crofts. Inspector French's search for the missing (and murdered) Sir John brings him from London by the overnight boat train "The Paddy" to Stranraer and The King's Arms for breakfast. Inquiries made by the indefatigable inspector of the receptionist at the aperture on the right yield valuable information about the movements of a suspect.

On shortest Sea route to Ireland. Entrance Hall, Kings Arms Hotel, Stranraer N.B.

The active involvement of the three principal members of the Stair family in the opening of Stranraer Lawn Tennis Club's resurfaced courts at Sun Street in 1906 is typical of their keen interest in community leisure facilities. This practical concern was demonstrated by the gift to the council of the land on which Stair Park with its abundant recreational facilities stands. Similarly the family gave to the burgh the ground near the seafront on which The Garden of Friendship was built and fields beside Cairnryan Road for a golf course. The Dalrymples of Stair came to Castle Kennedy in the mid-seventeenth century and in the next 100 years became the most powerful family in Scotland. The first two Lords Stair dominated Scottish legal and political life while the third gained renown on an even wider stage by becoming commander-in-chief of the British army and ambassador to France. The second Lord Stair's involvement in the Massacre of Glencoe and crucial role in the 1707 Union with England are unlikely to put his portrait on any Scottish banknotes.

The story of the numerous military installations in Wigtownshire in the two World Wars has been fully recorded but less attention has been paid to the measures taken locally to deal with their casualties. The use of local mansions for this purpose occurred in both conflicts. The unidentified stately home graced by two rampant lions at its main entrance was obviously a convalescent home in the First World War, when local efforts to ease the lot of the wounded were not confined to Wigtownshire: Lady Marjorie Dalrymple, sister of the 11th Earl of Stair, worked as a nurse close to the front line in the Ypres salient in northern Belgium on a canal barge converted into a mobile hospital, solaced by swapping copies of *The Wigtownshire Free Press* with an orderly. In the Second World War Lochnaw Castle near Leswalt became an RAF auxiliary hospital with 111 beds and three operating theatres. Galloway House at Garlieston was utilised for the same purpose, this time as a facility for both army and RAF personnel.

Leswalt Memorial Hall, built in 1927 to commemorate parishioners who died in The Great War, is not the only structure in the vicinity with martial connections. A mile to the west on the northern edge of precipitous Aldouran Glen stands a wedge-shaped fort defended by an impressive system of earth ramparts and ditches. Its name, Kemp's Graves, is significant for "Kempe" is the Anglo-Saxon and Norse word for a warrior and the name perhaps indicates an ancient local tradition of a Scandinavian presence here connected with the frequent Norse traffic up and down the Irish Sea. This may be the source of the village's name for one theory is that it comes from Gaelic and means "the fort of the glen". Another theory suggests an even earlier date for Leswalt's origins for it could mean "grass court/enclosure" and come from the earliest language found in local place names, British, language of the Britons and ancestor of Welsh. Whichever theory is correct, clearly today's unpretentious village has a long history.

The ruins of Leswalt old parish church are probably medieval for the village possessed a church in the mid-fourteenth century. However the venerable building is not showing its best side to the camera here for the rear, south-east corner with burial vault to the right is less than impressive. Much more deserving of photographic attention is the north side, dominated by the Agnew aisle, erected for the local landed family in 1644. Living members of the family made use of the lairds' loft upstairs while deceased Agnews were accommodated in the vault on the ground floor. Apart from its record of Agnew family history in the burial vault plaques, the aisle is noteworthy for the panel above the doorway with the arms of the normally feuding Agnews and Kennedies and above it the fine window illuminating the lairds' loft.

The Leswalt community obviously had a high regard for education as the village today boasts three buildings formerly or presently used as schools. The oldest, dating to 1776, is the large, much altered building standing immediately to the east of the old church. The church itself was pressed into service as a school for a time after its closure in 1828, probably while the school next door was undergoing alteration. With the introduction of compulsory education in 1872 a new school was built a quarter of a mile east at the crossroads. The small hut on its right was a paragon of versatility, serving as kitchen, dining hall, and classroom. Remarkably a painting of the 1776 school, "Leswalt Academy, Gallowayshire", by a former pupil hangs in the Boston Museum of Fine Arts. In the left background behind the wood the monument to Sir Andrew Agnew, 7th Baronet, keeps a watchful eye on the village.

With the mid-nineteenth century building of the new church and school at the crossroads, the centre of gravity of Leswalt moved eastwards along the Stranraer road. Thus at one time the post office was at the eastern end of the village close to Challoch Farm Cottages. The Leswalt version was typical of many local village post offices, consisting of the front room in a private house and offering a range of services. The left-hand notice informs locals they have access to the latest telecommunications technology, the telegraph. The window to the left of the door suggests this was also a shop while the pram and cycles outside could symbolise the use made of the place by the whole community, male and female, of all ages. It was therefore a valuable social centre and clearing house for local news.

Sea transport was as vital to the economy of the west side of Loch Ryan as it was to that of the west side of Luce Bay and for the same reasons. Soleburn, The Wig, and Lady Bay were all used by small coasting vessels with the best natural harbour at The Wig, "a secure anchorage in severe weather for small vessels" as it was justly described in *The (New) Statistical Account* of 1841. Lines of carts, Clydesdale-drawn, wait patiently to load their agricultural produce or take on lime or coal. However The Wig was not always used for peaceful purposes. The word is Scandinavian and means "small bay" while the name of the sheltering shingle bank on the north-east, The Scar, is also from Scandinavian. A thousand years ago the vessels on the beach here would have been Viking longships in passage to or from the Norse Irish Sea possessions. A sculptured stone, The Kilmorie Cross, now beside Kirkcolm Church, also confirms a Viking presence in the area.

Unlike neighbouring Leswalt and most villages in Wigtownshire, which "just grew", Kirkcolm, like Port William and Garlieston, is a planned village. After a false start in the early seventeenth century it was firmly established around 1780 by the owner of Corscwall estate, Stewart of Garlies, Earl of Galloway. He modestly named it Stewarton, a practice heavily criticised by Robert Burns as "christening kailyards" but posterity preferred to commemorate a saint rather than an earl. The village is literally at the gates of Corsewall House, built as a dower house but converted

to the laird's residence. The lodge guarding the main gate is visible above the second cart on the right. Lest the busy scene at The Wig gives the impression of "all work and no play" it should be recorded that the nineteenth century Kirkcolm winter was enlivened by farmers', small farmers', ploughmen's, and sailors' balls all held in Brown's Hall located on the first floor of the building immediately beyond the two-horse conveyance in the centre of the picture.

Kirkcolm Main Street in the early twentieth century presents a picture of unalloyed respectability but according to the parish minister things were very different in 1791 three years after the foundation of Stewarton/Kirkcolm. Rev. James McCulloch complains bitterly that of the 30 houses which then constituted the village more than one third were gin or whisky shops with consequent deleterious effects on the morals of the entire neighbourhood. When his wrath has subsided the minister records that most of the male population are tradesmen or farm workers. However at a later date Kirkcolm became noted as a nursery for sailors especially ships' masters, largely thanks to a private school where a whaling veteran taught the skills of seamanship. The village was also known as a centre for embroidering muslin webs, most of the young women being employed in this way.

Kirkcolm Smithy, an essential feature of any rural area for medical as well as agricultural reasons, was situated at the very top end of the village, the Dalkist Burn providing the essential water supply. Less than a mile upstream is a natural amphitheatre with a rock outcrop containing a man-sized cleft, which local tradition says was used as a pulpit by the famous Covenanting preacher Alexander Peden in the seventeenth century religious troubles. A wanted man for holding outdoor, illegal, Presbyterian services or conventicles, Peden spent most of his life on the run and the south-west is littered with "Peden's Pulpits". However it is very possible that this is an authentic example for the prophet occasionally had to seek refuge in Northern Ireland and Kirkcolm Parish is well endowed with secluded bays. Peden may have held one or more conventicles here going to or coming from Ireland; as former minister of New Luce he knew the area well.

Kirkcolm parish church occupies a commanding position on high ground on the west side of the village. looking directly across Loch Ryan at the village of Cairnryan just over two miles distant on the other side of the loch. This had interesting consequences during the ministry of one Rev. Marshall, a man endowed with a remarkable pair of lungs. He had already used them to good effect to blast out in a deafened state the mischievous ghost that had been harassing the residents of Galdenoch Castle. He achieved no similar feats at Kirkcolm but it was said that if the wind was in the right direction or absent his sermons could be heard without difficulty (or option) by the inhabitants of Cairnryan. On the west side of the church an enigmatic red sandstone statue, without inscription or identification, of a grieving woman and child, may commemorate the victim(s) of a local shipwreck.

The area at the southern end of Corsewall House policies beside the Boat Bank road entrance clearly justifies the claim of a 1908 guidebook that "many rare and flowering shrubs and trees grow in great luxuriance". It was in this part of the grounds that the tenth century Kilmorie Cross stood until almost decapitated by a falling tree. The benevolent Gulf Stream gives the Rhinns a climate ideal for growing rhododendrons and local landowners used to compete for excellence of display, helping to sponsor plant-hunting expeditions for new varieties and developing their own cultivars. As a result gardens like Logan, Ardwell, Dunskey, Lochinch, and Corsewall are still meccas for connoisseurs of the species.

Corsewall Mill, a mile north of Kirkcolm, was important enough for the highway to be realigned to run closer to the entrance. Traces of buildings behind the house at the roadside just to the south known as "Milton", probably the remains of a clachan, provide further evidence of the mill's significance. Corsewall was leased by the Hannay family in 1820 and they remained there for 70 years until their final move to Stranraer. The mill then closed. Dynamite, then a fire and eventual demolition, mean that the only trace remaining today is a set of millstones in a bridge parapet. At Corsewall the Hannays began the custom of sending a schooner loaded with bags of oatmeal for sale to the public up the west coast, the return cargo consisting of dried fish and slates. Girls on Islay wore the recycled oatmeal bags as dresses emblazoned on the front with "Hannays' Oatmeal". Was this the origin of the message-bearing tee shirt?

Strategically situated at the north-west corner of the Rhinns Peninsula, Corsewall Lighthouse was lit in 1816. It was built by Robert Stevenson, founder of the famous lighthouse-building dynasty, who was thus responsible for the lights at each end of the Rhinns Peninsula. Appropriately its signature is a light flashing red and white alternately for the builder invented flashing beams. The rubble walls are made of locally quarried whinstone but despite its hardness problems were encountered making the lighthouse watertight because the mortar in the joints did not adhere well to the whinstone. Mixing other ingredients with the mortar completely solved the problem and saved the reputation of local stone. A detailed account of the light mechanism, recycled from the Bell Rock Lighthouse, was provided by Robert Stevenson himself for the (*New*) *Statistical Account*.

Corsewall Lighthouse, Stranraer

Barney McGhies', near Kirkcolm

The name Portmullin for the small inlet half-a-mile east of Corsewall Lighthouse is a reminder that Barney McGhie's residence until his death in 1905 was originally part of a small, water-powered, meal mill. The aperture in the west wall for the millwheel drive shaft is hidden by the outcrop of rock. Despite the absence of visible water the presence of the boat reveals that local people used the inlet to fish for salmon and lobsters. Between Portmullin and the lighthouse a spring bubbling out of a grassy bank above the rocky shore is probably St. Columba's Well, which may or may not have any direct connection with the saint or his followers; it is certainly right on the North Channel seaways and the neighbouring inlet a welcome haven for storm-tossed travellers blown off their course. The holy well and its attendant wooden cross may have furnished the area with its name after deft transposition of two letters to make for easier pronunciation.

No settlement in Wigtownshire was more changed by the Second World War than the village of Cairnryan. Its previous name, from the Gaelic, "Macherie" or "Machiryskeed" (The Field of the Hawthorn) accurately describes its quiet charms and appeal to those seeking peaceful holidays with good seabathing. Its assets as a natural harbour were made little use of. However, between 1941 and 1943 the War Dept constructed here Military Port No.2 in case facilities on the Clyde were put out of action by enemy bombing. With three piers and 39 cranes, the new port could take the largest ship afloat. Not required for its original purpose, it was a major entry port for American troops and vehicles arriving in Britain for D-Day. After the war Cairnryan was used for dumping surplus ammunition and possibly even more sinister cargoes in the Beaufort Dyke in the Irish Sea. Ironically, after its nineteenth century rejection as Scottish terminus for the short sea route, the village now accommodates two harbours and two companies plying the passage.

Nestling in a glen above Cairnryan village, Claddyhouse contrarily has a Gaelic name meaning "The House on the Flat, Stony Beach". It has long been owned by the Dalrymple Hamiltons, relatives of the Stair family of Lochinch. Although it was originally a summer residence with the main house at Bargany near Girvan, Claddyhouse became the family home. The owner during the Second World War, Admiral Sir Frederick Dalrymple Hamilton, had a distinguished naval career. In 1941 he was captain of the battleship HMS *Rodney* in one of the best known engagements of that conflict, the pursuit and sinking of the German battleship *Bismarck*. One of the battle ensigns flown by *Rodney* that day now hangs in Inch Parish Church outside Stranraer. However the Admiral would probably have said that his command of five Russian convoys was a no less demanding assignment .

Prior to the post-Second World War construction of a model village bridging the gap, Dunragit consisted of two halves a few hundred yards apart. This eastern section faces the creamery, built on the site of Ballochjargon Starch Mill with its attendant burn. The name ("Dergan's Crossing" in Gaelic) suggests the original settlement grew up where the highway crossed the burn by a ford. Dunragit boasted the usual indispensable smithy, the building on the extreme right. The last occupants were the Duffy family, famous not only for their blacksmithing skills but also for their traditional-music-making abilities. The air of expectancy emanating from the assembled residents suggests the imminent passage through the village of an unidentified VIP. On the long straight over the brow of the hill on the left the A75 runs on the line of the Roman road from Glenlochar Fort near Castle Douglas to Loch Ryan, as proved by the existence of a line of small quarry pits on the south side of the road.

Dunragit Creamery was the first to be built in Galloway, opening in 1882. The Creamery Company was founded by Glasgow cheese wholesaler Andrew Clement and Wigtownshire farmer R. McCracken. The company soon expanded, building creameries at Sorbie and Colfin and changing its name to The United Creameries Ltd. By 1901 its portfolio of products included cream both in jars and in bulk, butter, margarine, and "exquisite cream cheese". It could boast a clutch of awards won at national events. The headhunting of several key personnel in 1907 by the newly opened Bladnoch Creamery and margarine factory does not seem to have been a mortal blow. The Dunragit plant was sold by United Creameries in 1921 to The English Margarine Company. Its final owner was the Nestle group, who manufactured condensed milk there. Small jars used for preserved cream from its United Creameries days, less ornately decorated that those of its Wigtownshire Creameries rival, can still be unearthed by the lucky browser in collectables shops.

The site of Dunragit Creamery was chosen because it was adjacent to the Stranraer-Dumfries railway and so its perishable products had access to a fast, nationwide, transport system. The creamery had its own siding but the village also had a station, its humble status emphasised by the fact that the decision to have a halt here was made only two months before the Stranraer-Castle Douglas line opened in March, 1861, and the provision of a wooden shed for passengers in lieu of a waiting room. However things changed in 1877 with the opening of the Girvan and Portpatrick Junction Railway, which joined the Stranraer-Castle Douglas/Dumfries line at Challoch Junction a mile east of Dunragit. The latter now became an interchange station for rail passengers from the Machars heading for Ayr, Glasgow, and beyond with consequent improvement of facilities to reflect its new status. Dunragit closed, a victim of Dr Beeching's cuts, in 1965.

The feature that gave Dunragit Station its initial name, "Genoch Level Crossing", went over the road in front of the light-coloured two-storey building facing the camera and in the vicinity of the foolhardy pedestrians. Station Road consisted of houses for railway employees required by the station's interchange role and the need for 24-hour manning of the signal box, which also controlled the level crossing gates. The end, two-storey house in the row was a tearoom necessitated by the station's new status. The station and its attendant buildings and population gave the village's western segment added importance and tilted Dunragit's centre of gravity to the west. Judicious scattering of Indian corn on the railway line followed by deft operation of the points lever from the signal box allowed the staff to present delighted visiting officials with pairs of neatly decapitated pheasants from the neighbouring estate.

Until the coming of the railway station, west Dunragit consisted of a scatter of estate workers' houses at the pillared entrance to the drive leading to Dunragit House half a mile uphill. The mansion was the seat of the Dalrymple Hays, owners for long of the Park-Dunragit estate. But close at hand may have been a much older power centre as the name Dunragit," The dun of Rheged", suggests. Rheged was one of the small British kingdoms which arose in the tumultuous years after the end of Roman rule in Britain around 410AD. One theory equates the territory of Rheged with Galloway and another claims that one of Rheged's kings, Urien, was the historical prototype of legendary British hero King Arthur of Round Table fame. If both are correct, then Dunragit as a main centre of Rheged may be Arthur's celebrated city of Camelot! Unfortunately the only physical evidence so far discovered of a site of the appropriate period is a fairly insignificant circular raised feature half way up the driveway but hope springs eternal …

A flock of sheep make an appropriate welcoming committee to New Luce for the valley north of the village is hill sheep country par excellence, sprinkled with farm names familiar in show ring and auction mart. New Luce stands at the junction of the Cross Water of Luce and the Main Water. The former comes in from the right to go under the bridge beneath the trees on the left and join its senior compatriot a hundred yards further on. The Main Water's course is roughly parallel to the main street above the bridge. As the village is also the centre of a network of secondary roads radiating in all directions it might be modestly termed a rural mini-communications hub. The surrounding countryside is dotted not only with sheep but with a wealth and variety of archaeological sites dating to prehistoric times. Many have evocative names like the Caves of Kilhearn, actually a chambered burial cairn, the Standing Stones of Laggangairn, and Cairn na Gath long cairn. The area is an archaeologist's paradise.

Like several other Wigtownshire clachans, New Luce has changed in the last 100 years from lively community to near-ghost village and then back again, the latter transformation as welcome as the former was regrettable. In its first incarnation, seen here, it boasted around 200 inhabitants by 1908 with at least one shop, on the left, and one of its two (formerly three) licensed premises in the right foreground. The Kenmuir Arms is named after an owner of that name, a Kirkcowan joiner who perhaps wished to give his hotel the same status as the rival Stair Arms, named after the area's principal landowner: the Gordons of Kenmure, who received a viscountcy from Charles I, were one of Galloway's leading families. The Kenmuir hotel appears, albeit under a slightly different name, in *Cold in the Earth*, a work of crime fiction by Aileen Templeton, much of which is set in the Luce Valley. As a counterweight to the Kenmuir Arms, the Free Church of Scotland building, partly visible above the horse-drawn van, stands at the end of the street.

The presence of three churches in New Luce in 1875 seems surprising but is a reminder of the important role of the church in nineteenth century Scotland and the intense feelings aroused by the Disruption of the Church of Scotland in 1840. The Free Church's spiritual rivals in the village were the parish church and a preaching station of the Stranraer congregation of the Reformed Presbyterian Church. The parish church had the advantage in terms of prestige as the only charge, from 1659 till his expulsion in 1662, of one of the giants of the Covenanting cause, Alexander Peden, "Peden the Prophet". So great was the awe in which he was held that in conformity with his parting injunction no Episcopalian minister entered his pulpit during the 26 years that elapsed before the restoration of Presbyterianism. The plethora of churches in New Luce in 1875 is also a reminder of how much more heavily populated even the moorland countryside was before the arrival of the internal combustion engine and especially the ubiquitous farm bike.

In Wigtownshire, as elsewhere in Scotland, the favourite sport of the farming community is curling. Before the advent of indoor ice rinks the game was played on lochs and ponds, natural or man-made, the latter being the case at Castle Kennedy, or on specially laid stretches of tarmacadam sprayed in frosty weather to produce the requisite ice. This cutting-edge technology was employed in Newton Stewart's York Road on the site of today's library, in Stranraer at Clashmahews on the town's southern outskirts, and improbably at the village of Whauphill. Because of the location of New Luce the Loch of Larg Curling Club, founded in 1841, enjoyed more opportunities for curling than most other clubs had. The artificial pond fed by the Pond Burn was situated on the north–west edge of the village between the Penwhirn road and the river. Former club members include a winner of the World Junior Rink Championship.

Glenluce Abbey, a few miles south of New Luce, was founded for the Cistercian order of monks in 1190 by Roland, Lord of Galloway. It gave hospitality to both King James IV and Mary, Queen of Scots, when they were on pilgrimage to Whithorn. On his 1507 visit the former gave a gratuity of four shillings to the gardener in appreciation of the excellent condition of the abbey gardens. The attractions for today's visitors are the finely restored chapter house and the remains of a state-of-the-art piped water system. Michael Scott, thirteenth century scholar and astrologer with a European reputation, is claimed on the flimsy basis of a supposed Southern Scotland connection to have been at one time a resident of the abbey. Viewed in the popular Scottish mind as a wizard he allegedly (and carelessly) left in a vault a library of "thousands of old witch songs and incantations, books of the black art and necromancy". In another vault he locked up the plague to prevent it devastating the local population.

'The tomb of "Young Lochinvar"' is in fact that of Abbot Robert Gordon, who died in 1548 after a tenure of office of only one year. The fact that he was a Gordon of Lochinvar as was the hero of Sir Walter Scott's poem of that name must have caused the optimistic misattribution. To aggravate the error, the Young Lochinvar of the poem is not what he seems. Scott based his work on an old ballad which exists in various versions. Some of those make no mention of Lochinvar while, horror of horrors, in others he is from the English side of the border. It seems as if a well known ballad was given a Galloway version with a prominent local personality as hero to enhance its local appeal The transformation could have been the work of Scott's fertile imagination or of an earlier, unknown minstrel. The impressively carved grave slab was discovered in the abbey's northern transept in 1899 during excavations.

The tower house Castle of Park occupies a commanding position on the banks of the River Luce close to its mouth. Built in 1590 by Thomas Hay and his spouse Janet MacDouall, its history is closely bound up with nearby Glenluce Abbey. Thomas was the son of Abbot Hay, who in 1560 conveyed the extensive and fertile abbey lands to Gilbert Kennedy, Earl of Cassilis, "ane very greidie manne and cairit nocht how he gat land ". It seems that in return Thomas or his family received a portion of the former abbey lands as a separate estate, on which the tower house was later built. Abbot Hay received much gentler treatment than the abbot of Crossraguel in South Ayrshire whom Gilbert had roasted on a spit to encourage him to transfer the Crossraguel lands to the Earl. The Hays continued to occupy the castle until around 1820, after the estate and neighbouring Dunragit estate had been united by marriage and a new laird's house built near the village of the latter name.

An unofficial encampment of travelling people close to Castle of Park and across the river from the substantial bulk of Bridge Mill is a forerunner of the present-day official travellers' site just east of Glenluce. The visual link between travellers and locality is a happy coincidence for the author of the Galloway classic *The Tinkler-Gypsies of Galloway*, Andrew McCormick, was a native of Glenluce. His book explains that the ceremony of divorce was performed in gypsy circles by the petitioner killing an animal in presence of his wife and declaring the appropriate words (for obvious reasons it would be inadvisable to quote them) over the corpse. Clearly the era of the "quickie" divorce had already dawned. Another Galloway book describes such a ceremony being performed near Glenluce on the Stranraer-Newton Stewart road, the unfortunate animal in this case being a horse bought for the purpose.

Bridge Mill of Park, the principal corn mill for the estate of that name, existed as early as 1695, ensuring the tenants were firmly thirled and liable for their multures. Astonishingly for a mill of its size, no trace of it is left today except for signs of the lade which brought water from the Rive Luce to power the impressive mill wheel. However the attractive mill house on the opposite side of the road is still occupied. According to tradition its predecessor was the scene of an altercation at the wedding of the miller's daughter. Young Hay of Park, enraged by a guest's suggestion that Hay's relationship with the girl had been closer than propriety required, fatally stabbed the offender, an action which resulted in his being declared an outlaw. He returned to the district disguised as a beggar and escaped detection.

Glenluce is situated where all the major east-west routes through Galloway (Roman road, military road, railway, A75) gingerly descended from the moors by way of the valley of the Lady Burn to cross the River Luce and reach the coastal plain. The village was formerly the service centre for a large agricultural area: in 1937 Glenluce could boast 21 shops and a branch of the National Bank of Scotland (the second building on the left). Prominent among retailers were the Henry family: the general stores in the left foreground reveal that by 1917 the Henrys were established in Glenluce while in 1927 three shops, a grocer, a draper, and a watchmaker, all bore the Henry name. The family were still commercially active in the village in the late 1940s. However their story is a microcosm of that of retailing in Glenluce and similar Wigtownshire villages. The explosion of car ownership in the second half of the twentieth century made for mobile consumers, attracted to larger towns to the often fatal detriment of local services.

Glenluce Public Hall, built in 1878, offers a wealth of useful information to the passer-by with a clock on the spire (invisible here) and more unusually a barometer beside the front entrance. The onlookers gathered to view the arrivals for the imminent event seem too sparse and the mailing date of 1914 for the postcard too late for this to be either the official hall opening or Queen Victoria's jubilee celebrations in 1887 and 1897. The police officer in attendance (bottom right) wears a cap devoid of the familiar black-and-white diced band introduced nationally in the 1930s and designed by Kirkcudbright artist Charles Oppenheimer, himself a special constable in the Second World War. The building on the left is part of the Henry retail empire while the lamp standard in front of it testifies to the existence of street lighting in the village.

Belying this peaceful scene, the Crown Inn (behind the pump with its lamp standard) was the scene in 1880 of a brutal unsolved murder when landlord James Milligan was fatally injured while trying to foil a robbery attempt. The elaborate pump was erected to commemorate the diamond jubilee of Queen Victoria in 1897. The white building at the top of the hill stands at the junction with North Street; the station was 100 yards up that street. Unlike Kirkcowan, Newton Stewart, and even more so Creetown, Gatehouse, and New Galloway, Glenluce Station was conveniently situated for the community it served. The King's Arms Hotel was thus able to boast "Three minutes from station" while the rival Commercial Hotel riposted "A few minutes walk from the station".

For the first fourteen years of its life Glenluce Station in North Street was very busy for the Wigtownshire Railway, serving the Machars, was not built until 1875 and the Girvan and Portpatrick Junction Railway down the Luce Valley came into service only in 1877. Glenluce therefore was the railhead for a large hinterland stretching from Whithorn and Port William in the south to New Luce in the north. Stationmaster James Nish must have earned his salary of one guinea per week plus rent-free house. The station was the scene of a bizarre accident in 1886 because the Stranraer-bound boat express was too long for the platform. Apparently unaware of the fact, a passenger in one of the carriages projecting beyond the platform stepped off the train and landed on top of a passing railway official, breaking the latter's leg. In our age of the compensation culture the results would have been far-reaching.

The old row of cottages on Main Street beyond the top of the hill has long since disappeared to be replaced by former local authority housing. They remind us of the settlement's original, fifteenth century, name Ballinclach, in Gaelic "The village of the stone buildings". The reference is probably to Glenluce Abbey further up the valley. The Gaelic name was replaced in the sixteenth century by the Scots "Clachan of Glenluce", shortened to Glenluce. The fifteenth century elevation of the village to burgh of barony status seems to have had few, if any, practical consequences. In a pleasant cameo Mr Gracie and his assistant pose at the door of the local convenience store while the cleaning of a cart, proceeding at a leisurely rate, has attracted an interested audience that spans the generations.

Main Street East, Glenluce.

Ladyburn U. F. Church, Glenluce

Ladyburn church occupied a secluded position south of the main street and close to the watercourse which provided its name. The story of the Presbyterian churches in Glenluce reflects the national story. Ladyburn was built in 1889 as a United Presbyterian church but when that body merged with the Free Church just eleven years later it became Glenluce United Free church until the 1929 union of the UF Church with the Church of Scotland. After the latter event it ceased to be a place of worship and became the local Masonic hall. The former Glenluce Parish was divided in 1647 into the parishes of Old Luce and New Luce. New Luce had its towering Presbyterian figure in the shape of Alexander Peden, but Old Luce had its luminary as well in the form of Glenluce-born Robert M'Ward, professor of philosophy at St. Andrew's university, friend of the great Samuel Rutherford, and exiled in Holland because of his support of the Covenanting cause.

Situated in the grounds of Balkail House on the edge of the Lady Burn Glen, Genzia's Well traditionally takes its name from a local tragedy as here a lady bearing that exotic name met an untimely fate, of which several versions exist. In one, Genzia was a servant at Balkail House who slipped and was drowned in the well while fetching water. In a more sinister variant the lady was murdered at this spot. One account pins the blame for the tragedy on the laird of Balkail, Sir John Dalrymple. Suspicious of his daughter's moral rectitude, he confronted her and struck her violently. The shattered girl left the house to spend the night out of doors and perish of hypothermia. You pays your money… What is beyond doubt is that for many years no self-respecting Glenluce youngster would venture near the spot after dark for fear of encountering Genzia's ghost.

According to well known travel writer George Borrow, who visited the village in 1866, the essence of the charm of Glenluce lay in "The glen, the little bridge, the rivulet and trees" all seen to advantage at Glenburnie Bridge, one of many traversing the "many-bridged Lady Burn" as it passes down its glen, a noted beauty spot. The buildings on the top left may be part of Balkail House, whose residents included Field Marshal Hew Ross, East India Company ship's master John Adair, and Colonel Barclay of Barclay's Bank. Purchased by the Earl of Stair in 1862, it was demolished in 1961, the site being now occupied by a caravan and camping site.

The location, size, and number of windows suggest that these houses close to the parish church in the oldest part of Glenluce may have been originally weavers' cottages. While the village was never an industrial centre, in 1869 the textile industry was modestly represented by two carding mills, one dye mill, and one flax mill, all powered by the lively waters of the Lady Burn. In 1654 a Glenluce weaver named Glbert Campbell achieved national fame as a result of his four-year harassment by the Devil of Glenluce. Apart from erudite, disembodied arguments with the minister and the quoting of Latin texts, the Devil employed himself gainfully and nocturnally by constantly slamming doors and cutting the hapless weaver's webs. These anti-social activities ceased after four years, encouraging theories that the Devil had more of the terrestrial about him than might have seemed to the credulous.

Glenluce is situated at the interface of the three divisions of Wigtownshire, the Rhinns, the Machars, and the Moors. Consequently it is a convenient location for events involving people or organisations from all over the former county. For indoor activities that function is fulfilled by the public hall, the large building with the clock tower in the left background. The hall's value in this role is recognised in a 1901 advert: "Accommodation 450. Open for Concerts and Dramatic Entertainments". It is interesting to speculate whether all the activities held in the building have fitted into one or other of those categories. The hall's equivalent for bowling is the Glenluce bowling green situated at the bottom of the Lady Burn Glen and much praised in guidebooks for the attractiveness of its location. Even at 1901 values the one shilling subscription for visitors seems not unreasonable.

Golf Clubhouse, Glenluce.

Glenluce Golf Club, founded in 1894, shares one asset with the marginally better known Gleneagles courses. In the railways' heyday both had their own station for the convenience of members and visitors. At Glenluce this comprised a wooden platform at Challoch Junction, half a mile distant, where on Wednesdays and Saturdays certain trains stopped to disembark and take on golfing passengers. A 1915 article also saw similarities between the nine-hole course itself and the historic Musselburgh links outside Edinburgh. Mention of a plethora of whins and wild roses lining the fairways and of the greens being natural suggests that at that time the venue had suffered little from the intrusive hand of man. In keeping with the strong Covenanting Presbyterian traditions of the area, in the late 1940s the club was the only one in Galloway not to permit Sunday golf.

Carscreugh Castle, situated on the moors four miles north-east of Glenluce, was the home of Ayrshire-born James Dalrymple, first Lord Stair, whose family was to dominate Scottish legal and political life for decades. He acquired the property through his wife, the formidable Margaret Ross of Balneil in the Luce Valley, in 1655 and built a tower house there. The remains are on the right. James Dalrymple, previously Professor of Philosophy at Glasgow University, became the foremost lawyer of his day and it was here that he wrote the legal classic *Institutions of the Law of Scotland*, still an authority on its subject. But his life at Carscreugh was shadowed by two domestic tragedies. In 1669 his daughter Janet, forced by her mother into a marriage contrary to her wishes, died in mysterious circumstances only four weeks after the wedding. And in 1682 his eldest grandson was accidentally shot and killed by his brother while the pair were playing with a visitor's pistol.

"Stairhaven," Glenluce

As the name indicates, Stairhaven Harbour was built by an Earl of Stair to provide harbour facilities on the exposed, inhospitable eastern shore of Luce Bay for his tenant farmers. Boats brought in cargoes of coal and lime and departed with agricultural produce. The local name for the place is the Craw's Nest, possibly originally the Cross Ness, "the cross on the headland". The use of the Scandinavian "ness" (headland) indicates we are now in Viking country while the "cross" may have some reference to the place name Kirkchrist in the vicinity. Lord Stair's pier has been reduced by the hostility of the prevailing westerly winds to a shapeless mass of rubble. Fortunately the same fate has not befallen an attractive stone-built, two-storey warehouse close by, erected for the convenience of local farmers using the harbour.

Situated at the foot of a wide, shallow depression running down to Luce Bay, the confusingly named clachan of Glen of Luce was the nucleus of a well populated area in the days of a more static rural population. Amenities included the Robert Burns public house (one of the two buildings in the left foreground), a post office cum general store , and a public school (both out of sight up the hill to the right). Had the ten houses planned by the county council in the 1950s been built, these amenities would have been fully stretched. In the same era the clachan enjoyed the services of a mobile bank. Those already puzzled by the local place name nomenclature may not wish to know that the school was known as Castle Daly…or that the clachan was sometimes known as Auchenmalg.

The Cock Inn or Cock of Luce Inn stands by the shore just south of Glen of Luce. Some locals say the name originated from the days when inns brewed their own beer. If the mix was not fermenting satisfactorily the landlord here would kill a cockerel and throw it into the brew to expedite the process. The Inn can claim a notable success story. Charles McClelland, born there when it was still a private dwelling house, emigrated to America after his apprenticeship in a Port William draper's ended abruptly in a row with his employer. In The United States he became in succession a lawyer, a Democratic member of The New York State Legislature and finally a judge in the United States Customs Court. Ironically the coast round Customs Judge McClelland's birthplace was in the late eighteenth and early nineteenth centuries a hotspot of smuggling activity and the inaccessible Smugglers' Cave on Sinniness Head just behind the Cock Inn an ideal warehouse.

Tower houses are fairly common in Wigtownshire but not so twin versions of the species. Such a one is Old Place of Mochrum in the moorland heart of the Machars. The fifteenth century Old (West) Tower is linked to the sixteenth century Red (East) Tower in a domestic extension of heroic proportions. In the late nineteenth century the towers, by now ruinous, were sympathetically restored and upgraded by two successive Marquesses of Bute, the owners, to create what one architectural critic has described as " a house of almost magical appeal". Another member of the family, younger son Lord David Stuart, after the Second World War made Old Place of Mochrum a centre of excellence for the breeding of Belted Galloway cattle. His work was continued and expanded by his daughter Miss Flora Stuart, who bred dun- and red Belties to complement the better known black variety. Her enthusiastic missionary work has much to do with the present popularity of the breed.

One of eight locations in Galloway bearing the name, Elrig Village in Mochrum Parish was in its heyday largely self-sufficient. It had a school, an inn, a joiner's workshop (possibly where the cart is parked), three dairies, and a smithy. In 1892 its population included a dancing master, a horse breaker, a shoemaker, and a tea dealer. Like New Luce and nearby Barrachan, social changes turned it into a near ghost village by the mid-twentieth century only for it to enjoy a regeneration twenty years later as a commuter and retirement location. In the 1960s the name Elrig became familiar nationally with the publication of the best seller *House of Elrig* by wildlife enthusiast and author Gavin Maxwell. The house so called is situated just over a mile north-west of the village and was Maxwell's birthplace and boyhood utopia. Locals often call the clachan The Lane after a Scots word for a moorland burn, in this case the one running down from Elrig Loch.

Built in the late eighteenth century on either side of the Elrig Burn just below the village, Elrig Mills were the largest in the Machars, comprising a bone-grinding mill, a meal mill, and a farina mill producing potato flour, a cheap and unpopular food. At their peak the mills had five water wheels and employed over 100 people. The bone-grinding function was of particular importance because the product provided fertiliser for the local farms and significantly improved agriculture in the area. Bones were shipped in to Port William to provide the raw material. For most of its active life the complex was owned by members of the well known Routledge family, who were responsible for its success. By the time it closed in 1913 the mill complex had found its way into Machars folklore, being the subject of two local sayings and a song "The Mochrum Bane Mill".

The first parish school was opened in Mochrum village in the 1720s but for a parish of forty square miles with a widely scattered population further provision was needed and eventually at various times public schools were opened at Port William, Elrig, the Dirrie (near Lochead of Elrig), the May (near Culshabbin), Greenhouse (beside the Rocks of Garheugh), and Culshabbin. As a result of rural depopulation and policy changes only Port Wiliam School has survived. This, the third, Mochrum school building was erected around 1830 and closed amid heated controversy in 1969, ending over 200 years of schooling in the Kirk Town. The story of education in the parish is similar to that of many other rural areas but Mochrum School almost had a notable claim to fame. In 1793 the Galloway-born linguistic genius Alexander Murray, then aged eighteen, optimistically applied for the mastership of the school. Rejected on the grounds of his youth, he took himself off to Edinburgh University and the consolation of an eventual professorship.

Unlike some other local villages Main Street in today's Mochrum offers little visual difference from the 1909 version. However, the latter offered an interesting juxtaposition. The building on the right facing the camera was until the late 1960s the George Hotel while 100 yards to its right behind the trees is the parish church. The arrangement may not have been disagreeable to the local residents. Sir Herbert Maxwell, laird of nearby Monreith estate, recollects in his autobiography that family members attending church service ensconced in the lairds' loft with its own fireplace would rattle the fire irons noisily when they felt the minister's sermon had run its proper course. An earlier landlord was the anonymous twelfth century Anglo-Norman lord who built his wooden castle at the northern end of Main Street. All that survives today is the motte, a prominent mound of earth like a gigantic, grassy molehill.

Port William was founded around 1770 by Sir William Maxwell of Monreith on the site of an existing small fishing settlement at the mouth of the Killantrae Burn. Although an 1875 writer dismissed the attendant harbour as "of the most primitive description" the new port flourished with the assistance of further harbour improvements by the Maxwell family. By the mid-nineteenth century twelve vessels were registered to Port William while in 1846 115 ships used the port. The pier facilities meant that the usual Wigtownshire agricultural exports could be augmented by farm animals while stones from the shore were dispatched to pave the streets of Liverpool. The number of stone-built warehouses on the quay tells a story of commercial success. Passengers were well catered for with regular services to both Glasgow and Liverpool, the latter provided by the famous iron paddle steamer *Countess of Galloway*.

The view of the landward end of the harbour clearly reveals its origins as a natural inlet at the mouth of a small burn, later diverted. The name of a well known local firm of agricultural suppliers adorns the gable of the warehouse on the right, testifying to the port's importance. Port William flourished until the arrival of the age of the internal combustion engine; the last commercial cargo landed was a load of coal from Ayr in 1942. Part of this scene is the subject of a crayon sketch by the celebrated Austrian Expressionist artist Oscar Kokoschka, who during the Second World War stayed on several occasions at House of Elrig, then the home of economist Professor Emil Korner. Parts of the local landscape appear in some of Kokoschka's best known paintings. Sadly his gifts of his work to local people were sometimes treated in cavalier fashion as the Expressionist style did not chime with local taste.

Originally and splendidly named The Noble Science Inn, the Monreith Arms hotel, on the left, benefited from the success of the harbour thanks to its adjacent position and had to be extended. It also enjoyed the benefits of another maritime connection. In an attempt to crack down on the rampant smuggling on the east side of Luce Bay in "The Happy Time" of the late eighteenth century, the authorities stationed a detachment of soldiers in Port William to aid the often outnumbered excisemen. The soldiers were accommodated in the Monreith Arms until a barracks was built for them in 1878 on the south side of the harbour. 1913 was obviously still the age of the horse and the single storey buildings on the right of the hotel were stabling. During the Second World War the Monreith Arms was one of three Machars hotels famous for the provision of sumptuous, pre-war meals at a time of austerity and rationing.

The Square was the main shopping centre of the village and on the south side along from the Monreith Arms were to be found W. Stewart's grocery business and the premises of Brown and Co., drapers and outfitters, the latter still in business on the eve of the Second World War. Stewart's very smart van is a reminder that until the post-war era most country people travelled little and so the shops had often to go to the customer firstly in the form of the itinerant packman then the horse-drawn van and finally its motorised successor. On the side of his van Mr Stewart favours the one-word form of the village's name; others favour the two-word version and the question which is the proper form is a perennial subject of lively local debate.

A reminder that even in the age of near-universal car ownership the mobile shop survives in some rural areas. The grocer's van appears to have gone but until recently fruit and, as seen here, butcher meat were sold from mobile units and in the Machars fish vans still operate widely. It is significant that all items sold are perishable foodstuffs.

The eighteenth century Port William meal mill, of three storeys with warehouses, occupies the east side of the Square but just manages to sneak into the picture. Originally powered by the water of the Killantrae Burn, it was later converted to electricity, finally closing in 1982. For most of the nineteenth century it was owned by the Routledge family, who also owned the Elrig mill complex. The large building in the centre opened in 1864 as a branch of the City of Glasgow Bank, with agent's house (the agent was a member of the ubiquitous Routledge family). After the failure of that institution in 1878 it was taken over by the British Linen Bank, later absorbed in the Bank of Scotland. In the mid-twentieth century the agent's house was the boyhood home of joint winner of the Nobel Prize for Economics Professor James Mirrlees. He was awarded the coveted honour in 1996.

The eastern extremity of High Street on the plateau above the hill was intended as Port William's transport hub. When the Wigtownshire railway from Newton Stewart to Whithorn was opened in 1875 a six-mile branch line was proposed from Whauphill to Port William at a cost of £25,000. Unlike similar situations elsewhere in the area the local laird, Sir Herbert Maxwell not only did not oppose the plan; he offered to pay half the cost. Sadly the scheme never went ahead. However, in expectation that it would, an optimistic developer called Clephan built the first house on the right, Seymour House, to serve as the railway hotel, the Turnberry Hotel of the Machars. The first house on the left, with its gable to the road, was the original City of Glasgow Bank branch in the village.

Main Street, running north from the Square, was a multi-function thoroughfare. At the south end it was a continuation of the village's shopping centre but its northern end, out of sight round the corner, had an uninterrupted view of the bay and there were situated the villas of some of the village's leading citizens. In between were two prominent buildings. On the left the largest building in the street was the Eagle Hotel, in the immediate post-war era enjoying a reputation for food rivalling the Monreith Arms. Diagonally across and concealed behind the street front buildings was the United Presbyterian Church, later converted to secular use as the Maxwell Hall, the village's centre of community activities. At the edge of the village a natural pool by the shore, the circular Fluke Hole, was converted to a bathing pool with two changing rooms provided for the maintenance of modesty.

Main Street is littered with clues about Port William's role as a holiday resort. One such is the confectionery shop and tearoom of Miss Grace Stewart close to the Eagle Hotel. Miss Stewart, presumably the formally attired lady at the door, was involved in both the wholesale and retail sides of the confectionery business. Indications of such a demand for sweeties speaks 'holiday resort'. The existence of the Eagle Hotel and a bathing pool, albeit outdoor and unheated, provides further evidence. In fact the village has a long history in that role: a 1901 guide claims that it has "all the requisites for making holidays easy, health-giving, and enjoyable". And in the 1930s a direct bus service ran between Glasgow and "the Port" particularly for the benefit of Glasgow Fair holidaymakers flocking to the resort. The first 60 years of the twentieth century were the boom years but now the allure of Luce Bay has been dimmed by that of balmier climes.

The most popular summer game in Wigtownshire, appealing to all ages, both sexes, and every sector of society, is traditionally green bowls. Almost every town and village possesses its green, invariably beautifully tended, and, especially in the villages, often acting as a social centre. In winter devotees switch comfortably to the indoor version. No longer played appears to be the outdoor game of quoits, demanding a formidable combination of strength and skill and always pronounced "kites". Formerly quoiting rinks existed at Bladnoch beside the road bridge, at the south end of Kirkcowan, and close to the tennis courts at Port William. Across the road from the tennis courts, beside the school, Port William Bowling Club opened in 1872 on ground given by Sir Herbert Maxwell, seventh baronet of Monreith. Sir Herbert, a polymath with a national reputation as author, historian, archaeologist, horticulturalist, and natural historian, thereby added to his credentials as a generous benefactor of the village founded by his grandfather.

The area round Port William exhibits an astonishing number of examples of a type of monument associated with the people who lived in the Bronze Age between four and five thousand years ago. This is the cup-and-ring rock with an infinite combination of the two elements incised on rocky outcrops. Their purpose remains unknown although one book on the subject enumerated almost 100 possibilities. All that can be conservatively said is that they were probably carved for ritual purposes ; fevered speculation about human sacrifices with a sanguinary purpose for the cups and rings is best ignored. Drumtroddan Farm two miles north-east of Port William is an ideal place to view those enigmatic creations as it offers car parking, easy access, and interpretation panels. It also offers close by a fine example of another type of Bronze Age monument in the shape of a setting of three standing stones, unusually for Wigtownshire tall and slender unlike the more usual rounded boulders of a site like Torhousekie outside Wigtown.

One of the most popular beaches in the Machars has always been the Black Rocks on Monreith Bay, traditionally a favourite spot for Sunday school picnics. The sprinkling of holiday houses behind the beach is further testimony to its appeal. The nearest house, almost in the middle of the picture, is a recycled auxiliary classroom from the agricultural training centre for orphan boys established at Craigeach close to Old Place of Mochrum by the third Marchioness of Bute. During the invasion threat of 1940 the beach was identified as a very likely landing place for German troops, either waterborne or, at low tide, airborne. With inadequate manpower, the only form of defence was thought to be stakes driven into the beach. Although this was not done, poles were driven into the verge on the longest straight stretch of road between Barsalloch Point and Port William creamery to prevent glider landings.

Despite its idyllic appearance Monreith was a small-scale industrial village with a tileworks, established by the estate, and two industries powered by the Monreith Burn. The first, close to the road at the foot of the village, was a textile, probably waulk, mill and the other, almost on the shingle at the mouth of the burn, a grain mill hence the settlement's Sunday name Milltown of Monreith. The obligatory smithy was occupied for a time by the legendary blacksmith John McNeillie, dominant figure in a series of books published by his grandson, bearing the same name but writing under the pen name of Ian S. Niall. Hidden behind the houses at the bottom of the row is the village hall, donated to the community by Sir Herbert and Lady Maxwell. In 1881 it was the subject of a heated controversy about whether a woman should be allowed to give a lecture there.

The bus ambling towards the south end of Monreith past John McNeillie's Clarksburn Smithy is a reminder that even at its fullest extent the railway network did not cover substantial parts of Wigtownshire, particularly the west Machars and the south Rhinns peninsula. The gap was filled by bus services. The large Caledonian Omnibus Company, part of a national organisation, linked the main towns from 1927 but the smaller villages were served by a multiplicity of local companies, for example McKeand of Newton Stewart and his Kirkinner namesake, McLean of Port William, Bell of Wigtown (one bus, two scheduled services), and McCutcheon of Kirkcowan. In the Rhinns the rural roads were alive with the sound of Murray's buses in their familiar blue livery. Some of those companies offered remarkably high standards of service: McLean's Friday run to Newton Stewart livestock market carried unaccompanied calves.

KIRKMAIDEN / GLASSERTON PARISH WAR MEMORIAL

Twining itself round the grassy Point of Lag, Kirkmaiden golf course enjoys a spectacular situation. The Well Hole with the distance from tee to green better measured in terms of altitude rather than length is one where in the words of a 1915 guide "great skill is needed to avoid disaster". The Back Bay beyond is a favourite beach while the well itself is at the foot of the rocks on the left. The Front Bay on the other side of the point may be less popular for bathers and picnics but the well at the foot of the headland beyond the old church easily surpasses its neighbour in glamour. It miraculously appeared to aid the saintly Irish princess Medana in her hour of need. Her flight from an importunate suitor took her here from Ireland via Kirkmaiden-in- Rhinns and when her admirer pursued her she tore out her eyes and flung them at him. After his remorse-stricken departure a spring burst from the rock, its water restoring her sight.

The war memorial for Glasserton Parish enjoys a rural, sylvan setting opposite the main entrance to Glasserton House, Robert Adam-designed but now demolished, and the parish church. The monument was dedicated in 1920 by Sir Herbert Maxwell, Lord Lieutenant of the county and a long-serving officer with the Ayrshire Militia. The impressive display of regimental uniforms by the official party probably testifies to Sir Herbert's influence. Particularly appropriate is the presence of two naval officers for in the late eighteenth century the Glasserton estate was owned by Keith Stewart, a younger son of the Earl of Galloway, who after a career of much active service including the Relief of Gibraltar in 1782, rose to the rank of Vice-Admiral. The nursing volunteers on the left are a reminder of the major contribution of women to the conduct of the First World War.

75

St Ninian's Cave at the north end of Port Castle Bay on the west coast of the Machars has always been associated with fifth century St. Ninian, the first Christian missionary to Scotland. It is generally believed that the saint used it as a retreat after the example of the famous monastery of St. Martin at Tours: evidence suggests a link between the two saints. Its consequent popularity with pilgrims to St. Ninian's shrine at nearby Whithorn may result from the bay being a convenient landing place, avoiding the often forbidding waters round Burrowhead and offering a convenient route by Physgill Glen to their final destination. Less spiritually motivated travellers in more recent times have included fishermen and smugglers. Happily the tradition of pilgrimages to the cave has lived on.

The evidence for early and continuing visits by pilgrims to St. Ninian's Cave takes the form of numerous crosses, some carved on the cave walls and some on pieces of loose stone. The oldest ones are incised using the pocked technique employed on early Christian memorial stones. The crosses range in age from the seventh to the eleventh centuries and several exhibit characteristic features of the famous Whithorn school. A paving slab from the floor turned out to be a reused eleventh century grave slab inscribed in Anglian (Anglo- Saxon) and perhaps erected to a member of the Whithorn monastic community who chose to adopt the hermit's life. The crosses carved on loose stone are now on display in the Historic Scotland museum at Whithorn.

In St. Ninian's Cave the difficulty of locating genuinely old carvings and distinguishing them from natural features and more modern human creations is very clear despite the poor quality of the photograph.

W. 17. *Rock incised with Celtic Crosses, St. Ninian's Cave, Whithorn.*

The view of Isle of Whithorn from Tonderghie Road amply confirms the 1847 *Gazetteer of Scotland*: "The harbour is well sheltered and safe and possesses internal spaciousness". Where the account seems erroneous is in its reference to the bay "being almost landlocked by an islet" for to modern eyes no islet is to be seen. However, for centuries the village lived up to its name. The islet, wonderfully named "Inner Kirk of the Isle" in a 1750 map, was indeed one at high tide but at low tide it was linked to the mainland by a bar or isthmus of sand and gravel. Around 1800 man took over from nature's leisurely engineering and turned the shingle bar into a permanent causeway eventually with houses. The area from the white church projecting into the harbour to the two storey-building facing us on its right is where the water flowed at high tide. Sceptics should stroll down the lane diagonally opposite the church and read the reminiscences of Willie McCulloch, grandson of the last ferryman.

The village today may be a picturesque backwater, but in the days of the primacy of sea transport up till the mid-nineteenth century and the railway age Isle of Whithorn was at the heart of the national transport system situated as it was at a major intersection on the main north-south highway up the west side of Britain. It is no wonder that the 1847 *Gazetteer* commented that the Isle had "external advantages of position which might ...be turned to patriotic and lucrative account." In confirmation the 1841 *Statistical Account* reports that small vessels (like the topsail schooner on the right) sailed weekly to Whitehaven and other English ports and that the harbour was visited by the steamer *Countess of Galloway* on her way to and from Liverpool.

Isle of Whithorn did not merely accommodate ships; from at least 1800 it also built them. One of the best known shipbuilders was the McWilliam family. Their yard was situated on the shore between the church and the landward end of the quay and by 1851 they had a workforce of eight. The loss of a valuable cargo led to the closure of the business but the family used the remaining timber to build on the same site the famous leaning shop, a celebrated village landmark now sadly demolished. The

boatbuilding tradition was continued into more modern days: Alan Faulds built vessels often of fibre glass in a workshop close to the old McWilliam yard. Names of Isle boats tended to fall into three categories: local place names (*Cutcloy*), well known local residents (*Sir William Maxwell*), and names with personal and domestic associations (*Jane and Mary*).

The village did not only build ships; it bred sailors. The three McGuire brothers seen here, members of a seafaring dynasty, spent their lives apart from naval service inshore fishing in the local area. The target of the local inshore fisherman is usually lobsters but the boats used seem perilously small to be flirting with the jagged rocks, where the creels have to be set as close in as possible. Further complications can arise from unexpected and unwelcome occupants of the creels: crabs, conger eels, and jellyfish slime. The work is not only dangerous but hard with creels to be hauled once a day along several miles of coastline from spring to the onset of winter in all kinds of weather. It is not surprising that the inshore fisherman, especially the lobster fisherman, is a disappearing breed nor is it surprising that the job produces seamen of outstanding quality.

Populated by an abundance of fine sailors and surrounded by an equal abundance of stretches of implacably hostile coast, Isle of Whithorn was an obvious location for a lifeboat station and one was established in 1869, the first boat being the *Charlie Peak*, named after a relative of the donor. The lifeboat house was cleverly situated on the edge of an isthmus on the peninsula south of the village so that she could be launched into the west bay or the east bay depending on the wind direction. This was an important factor as all three boats based at the Isle were powered by oars with some assistance from a small sail. After 25 launches and 38 lives saved the station was closed in 1919, when the Kirkcudbright lifeboat took over responsibility for the area.

Despite the ample size of the wheels on the launching bogie, hauling the lifeboat from shed to shore was clearly a strenuous activity demanding a large launching crew and it was probably recruitment problems for this vital task that contributed to the demise of the station. The unco-operative terrain suggests that this launch is taking place to the east bay. Another vital task was administering and financing the station and the committee charged with those tasks in 1911 included some well known names from the professional and farming community: H. Johnston Stewart, John Black, Alex Macfie, J. McLean, G.A. McIlwraith. Almost inevitably one of the crew was called McGuire. It is possible that this is the second boat, *Henry and John Leighton*.

The station's final boat *George and Margaret* reassuringly afloat in the east bay (Chapel Port). The figures in the left foreground suggest that the cause of equal opportunities made an early appearance in the South Machars. The building in the background is much older than the nearby lifeboat house. The thirteenth century St. Ninian's Chapel has been claimed as the first church established by the saint, but modern scholarship grants that honour to nearby Whithorn and sees this building as a chapel where seaborne pilgrims en route for the saint's shrine at Whithorn Priory could give thanks for their safe arrival. The chapel's appearance was somewhat compromised in the nineteenth century when the dressed stone surrounds of the windows and doors were removed for inclusion in a new house in the village, a piece of recycling not without precedent in neighbouring Whithorn. It was restored in 1898 to the state seen here by the Marquess of Bute, whose local restorations did not always have such happy results.

The belated arrival of the railway from Newton Stewart at Whithorn in 1877 certainly weakened the Isle's maritime connection commercially but by no means ended it. The war memorial for the village and district, happily situated in the grounds of the bowling green, bears on its 1914-18 panel twelve names, five of whom served in the navy. One of the fallen served in the remarkable hybrid Naval Division, formed at the outbreak of war from naval reservists for whom no ships were available. To their surprise they were converted because of military manpower shortages into an infantry battalion and fought as such during the entire war, retaining all the outward features of a naval unit. One of their battalion commanders, drafted from the Grenadier Guards, was Aymer Maxwell of Monreith, son and heir of Sir Herbert and father of naturalist Gavin. He was killed by a shell a few hours after the force landed in Belgium in October, 1914, to defend Antwerp. The memorial was dedicated in 1921 by Sir Herbert.

Bysbie Mill, tucked discreetly behind the Queens Arms hotel, probably dates from 1817, the date engraved on the millstones. It succeeded an earlier version as the estate mill for the barony of Bysbie (Busby), to which all tenants were thirled in the customary way. Water power came via a mill dam from the Drummullin Burn. The mill passed into private hands but was still in use in 1945. This attractive scene was recorded by well known Kirkcudbright artist E.A Taylor in a painting now in the Kelvingrove gallery in Glasgow. Sadly the dam and mill wheel have gone and the mill is seriously derelict. The name "Bysbie" indicates a Scandinavian chapter in the village's early history. The lands bearing that name were eventually absorbed into Tonderghie estate.

Relieved of its mill-driving duties the Drummullin (Gaelic "ridge of the mill") Burn potters happily to the sea under the Physgill Row bridge, with the castle in the left background. Mill, castle, and burn were probably the core of early mainland Isle of Whithorn. Two-storey Laigh Isle House suggests the village at least at times enjoyed a degree of prosperity: in 1852 residents included four shoemakers, six grocers, four innkeepers, two master mariners, two shipbuilders, and a cabinetmaker. Beyond Laigh Isle House the junction with the Portyerrock road was known as Tru (through) Gate End before many of the colourful local names were regrettably culled in the late nineteenth century. Across the junction the first (last?) cottage in the former Glasserton Row has like its fellows given way to a car park. The unexpected cart and horse on the beach may be collecting seaweed for fertiliser.

Many, perhaps most, Scottish "castles" are in fact tower houses, fortified domestic residences built from the fifteenth to the seventeenth century in response to the lawlessness and insecurity of those troubled times. At least 150 were constructed in Galloway. Isle of Whithorn Castle was built towards the end of the period, in 1674, by Patrick Houston of Drummaston, at a time when greater internal law and order meant the concentration was more on comfort than security. However, the consequent lack of defensive features hardly justifies a recent writer's description of it as "Patrick Houston's villa". The suggestion that some of the architectural features show an Irish influence is a fascinating one, given such links are more associated with the Rhinns. In the early eighteenth century the castle was the home of Sir John Reid, Superintendent of the Coast Guard, who suffered his worst humiliation at the hands of his smuggling adversaries in the bay at his front door.

Whithorn, a royal burgh since 1511, is fortunate to retain almost intact the typical street plan of a medieval burgh. The near rectangular shape of the old town was dictated by the need to make the main street wide enough to accommodate a market and also seal both ends so that comings and goings could be monitored and regulated. At the far end of the street can be glimpsed part of the short transverse row of houses which performed the latter function, allowing a small gap or port which could be closed by a gate. The more distant curve in the street may have been dictated by the course of the burn which crosses the road here, now in a culvert, and the nearer by the need to ease the gradient for north-bound vehicles. The comment in Fullarton's 1847 *Gazetteer* that the street possesses "needless and vacant spaciousness" appears to miss the point but almost redeems itself by praising the "beautiful little stream of water spanned by a good bridge" which runs across the main street.

Whithorn's multifunctional tolbooth, essential symbol of burgh status, stood originally in the middle of the street at its lowest point, a location also chosen for its peers at the other royal burghs of Wigtown and Stranraer. It was eventually demolished and replaced by the building with the tower and spire on the right, the Old Town Hall, which still stands. The gate pillars beyond the second building on the right indicate the line of the now subterranean Ket Burn. The south port, happily still surviving despite its effect on modern traffic flow, is almost visible at the top of the hill. The animated scene is the result of the return home of the annual parish church picnic, several of the farm carts and horses which provided the transport being clearly visible.

The unprepossessing remains of thirteenth century Whithorn Priory do little to suggest its former splendour and prestige. The great cathedral priory (abbey in all but name thanks to ecclesiastical protocol) stood on or near the site of a series of religious buildings beginning with St. Ninian's fifth century white church of stone *candida casa* and including a Celtic and a Northumbrian monastery, the former a famous seat of learning where St. Columba's tutor was educated. As the priory housed the shrine and relics of St. Ninian, for centuries it was the most important pilgrim destination in Scotland, attracting a procession of monarchs from Robert the Bruce to Mary Queen of Scots with James IV visiting with almost embarrassing frequency. The foreground paved area is probably the site of the altar with the building on the left being the nave. Transepts and crossing have been replaced by part of the churchyard while the 1822 parish church on the right stands on the site of the cloisters.

Whithorn Priory was the architectural equal (and spiritual superior) of the famous Border abbeys but the only substantial surviving evidence is this doorway at the west end of the nave. It has a complicated history being in fact a hybrid of two separate twelfth century doorways, neither of which originally stood here. When the nave of the priory became Protestant cathedral then parish church after the Reformation this doorway was inserted to make an impressive entrance. Unfortunately the effect was spoiled by the addition of a porch, the inverted-V roof slot for which sadly disfigures the fine carving. Careful study of many houses in the main street will yield smaller examples of carved stonework of priory origin.

Beyond Port Mouth at the north end of Main Street (now George Street) the road narrows to become St. John Street leading to the station and the creamery, both out of sight round the bend in the road. This was an area of late nineteenth and early twentieth century development with the above buildings being joined by a new town hall, a prison, and a public library, the latter partly financed by joint founder of the Esso Petroleum Company local man Charles Lockhart. Just visible above the horse and cart is "Oswie" villa, built at the same period of expansion by James Duff, Isle of Whithorn-based grain and general merchant and ship owner, who serviced the firm's branches at Port William, Garlieston, and Wigtown by his own steamer the *Vanderbilt*. The business was eventually sold to well known local firm James Wyllie and Sons.

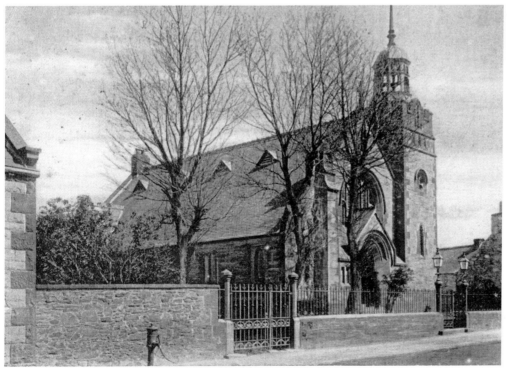

Like the Ladyburn Church in Glenluce the church site in St. John Street encapsulates the complex history of Presbyterianism in Scotland since the eighteenth century. Built as a Secession Church in 1793, it became successively United Presbyterian, then United Free, redundant after the latter joined with the Church of Scotland in 1929, and secularised firstly as a grain store and latterly as a garage. Along the way a new building was erected in 1892; the "dumpy battlemented tower" which aroused the ire of one architectural critic is still there but the circular appendage surmounting it has gone. To have a church and street named after St. John appears odd in a town dominated by St. Ninian. The explanation probably is that property in the neighbourhood once belonged to the Order of St. John of Jerusalem. That is certainly the reason for a similar case in Stranraer.

When the Wigtownshire Railway was proposed to serve the eastern Machars, the intended termini were Newton Stewart and Whithorn. However for financial reasons when the line opened in 1875 it ran only to Millisle with a spur to Garlieston. It was almost two years before capital was obtained to take the railway all the way to Whithorn to the delight of the populace:

> What gudes we noo may hae to spare,
> Be't kintra growth or merchant ware,
> Is sure to find a sale somewhere -
> Thanks to the Wigtown railway.

A proposal to continue the line to Isle of Whithorn by a tramway running mostly on public roads did not find favour. At one time it was possible to leave Whithorn Station with its single platform and travel to Edinburgh in the same carriage. However a degree of casualness in running the line was shown by an incident outside Whithorn in 1885 when the fireman fell from the engine without the driver noticing but fortunately also without fatal consequences.

Whithorn Creamery was built in 1914 by the Scottish Co-operative Wholesale Society. Like many others it had piggeries attached to it, the occupants feeding on the whey which was a by-product of cheese making and which otherwise was difficult to dispose of. In the early days farmers usually sent their own milk into the unloading bay, here on the left. The morning milk run by spring cart or dray became a hotly contested race with every driver regarding it as a matter of honour not to be overtaken, regardless of the effect on his cargo while the creamery workers watched the proceedings with interest. Later the creameries organised a milk collection service using steam wagons or steamers, whose solid rubber tyres were not beneficial to the untarred roads. Farmers using the service had to erect a wooden platform at the farm roadend for ease of handling the milk churns.

Whithorn became a destination for large numbers of immigrants from Ireland in the nineteenth century, a fact which greatly distressed the parish minister. In 1839 in a complaint familiar to our modern ears he claimed the influx caused an excess of labour supply over demand and so depressed wages. Many of the new arrivals settled in High Street beyond High or Isle Port Mouth. It may have been this that accounted for the presence of a Roman Catholic meeting house in the area and the existence of Townhead public school just behind the photographer where the road divides. Meeting house and school have long gone but the Calcutta Inn, established in the late 1880s, is still with us.

Because of Cruggleton Point's commanding position and excellent natural defences, the successive ruling powers of the area had a presence there from the first century A.D. to the late seventeenth. They included Celts, Anglo-Saxons, Scandinavians, and the medieval Lords of Galloway. Colourful traditional tales tell how a Norse attempt to capture the stronghold from its local garrison involved the treacherous and sinister Boatman of Cruggleton with his enchanted raven banner. The failure of the plan contrasted with the castle's successful capture by William Wallace from its English garrison in the days of Edward I. With the aid of Cruggleton's rightful owner McCairill, the great patriot climbed the precipitous sea cliffs, slew the sentries, and opened the gates to his waiting band, who made short and lethal work of the garrison. The only sizeable fragment visible today is part of the barrel vault of the later stone castle, the latter pictured in a sixteenth century print. The site with its spectacular strata is threatened by erosion.

The Lookout, a miniature echo of Cruggleton castle and situated a mile to the east, is located on the popular coastal walk west from Rigg Bay towards Cruggleton Point. According to an 1875 guide balconies had been formed at the top of some of the highest cliffs, thus giving walkers the opportunity of "peering over the rude rail to look down on a tremendous 100' precipice." Less adventurous souls could use the tower as intended to enjoy the panorama of the Stewartry coast. Another attractive feature of the Galloway House policies was the excellent collection of shrubs and trees planted by the seventh earl, founder of Garlieston. But his efforts were surpassed in the early twentieth century by celebrated gardener Neil Mac

THE LOOK OUT, CRUGGLETON, GARLIESTOWN.

Eacharn, who applied his talents to the woodland gardens before selling Galloway House and moving to Italy, where he established the internationally famous gardens at the Villa Taranto on Lake Maggiore.

14 GARLIESTOWN HARBOUR FROM SOUTH ST.

The sight of the Liverpool steamer manoeuvring at the foot of Garlieston's South Street illustrates how closely the village's story is intertwined with the sea. The first settlement on the site was a fishing clachan called Carswell situated on the south side of what is now Garlieston Bay at the mouth of the Broughton Burn. About 1760 John, Earl of Garlies, later the seventh Earl of Galloway, built here a planned estate village to complement the nearby family seat, Galloway House. With harbour facilities added Garlieston prospered as a well positioned Irish Sea trading and ferry port. In a curtailed form this role survived the arrival of the Wigtownshire Railway in 1875. In the Second World War Garlieston made a vital contribution to Allied success as the service port for the trials of the three competing versions of the famous Mulberry transportable harbour crucial to the success of the D-Day invasions. The trials took place along the coast between Garlieston and Whithorn because of its tidal similarity to the Normandy coast.

The natural harbour (out of shot on the right) though tidal, according to the usual Solway custom, was soon expanded by the addition of a pier in 1838, a stone breakwater in 1843 and a further pier extension in 1853. These ushered in Garlieston's boom era. Its geographical situation made it the busiest Wigtownshire port in the regular service between the Solway harbours and Liverpool, which was as important for livestock as for human passengers. The paddle steamer taking off at a great rate in the left background is probably the iron-hulled version of *The Countess of Galloway* heading for the Mersey. The vessels alongside the pier prove an active involvement in the Irish Sea trade: in 1838 fifteen vessels belonged to the port with four capable of carrying 100 tons. However the internal combustion engine completed the work the railway had begun and Garlieston's days as a commercial port have long gone.

The most attractive feature of Lord Garlies's street plan for his village is the gently curving crescent following the shoreline of the bay. Somewhat unexpectedly it was divided into two by a large grain mill powered by the waters of the Dowalton Burn. The building in the background gable-on to the street replaced an earlier mill burned down in 1889 and has itself now been demolished, leaving a water wheel as proof of its existence. The wheel symbolises how much the village economy depended on the processing and transportation of grain, a fact emphasised by the stone-built granaries on the quay but no longer by the huge, modern, redbrick mill, also demolished, on the waterfront beside them. The small brick building in the middle of the picture is the bowling club pavilion in winter garb. The street water pump in the right foreground shows that the era of gravitation water has not reached the village but by way of compensation the fine lamp standard proves it has street lighting.

Behind the seafront crescent Garlieston had a gridiron street plan, High Street being the western extremity. It perhaps bears that designation less happily than some of its earlier titles: Thatched Row, West Street, Heigh Row, with variants. In 1915 John Hannah, who ran the posting establishment attached to the Queen's Arms Hotel, was hedging his bets on the future of land transport by offering all branches of posting and also a motor car for hire. Presumably previous hotel proprietor H. Evans was not the party referred to in licensee Marshall Young's advert of the same year announcing with heavy significance "Under New and Capable Management". Despite his strategically advantageous position at the road entrance to the village Mr. Young faced stiff competition from the Galloway Arms in South Crescent, which smugly advertised "Patronised by all the Leading Families in Galloway". A lodge just beyond the far end of the street suggests the Galloway family were anxious to keep in close contact with their creation.

High Street was well served by licensed establishments with one at each end. The loyalist Queen's Arms at the north must have felt uneasy about the proximity of its southern equivalent the Smugglers' Arms but perhaps happier with the latter's later title of the Masonic Arms. The street in the foreground going down to the right, South Street, seems at varying times to have been the location of most of the village's essential services for over the years it has accommodated the post office and telegraph station, a doctor's surgery, a highly regarded private school known as Pogue's School, and the police station with attendant cells, not forgetting Mrs Dally's Cyclists' Rest Tea Rooms. A "pop-up" bank branch, open once a

week in a private house, was located just round the corner. Garlieston was fortunate with telecommunications for it had the penny post by 1838 and a wireless telegraph station by 1871. On the other hand the 1852 arrival time for the mail of 9p.m. and collection at 2a.m. seem less than totally convenient.

The square is situated rather unusually at the south-east corner of the village close to the junction of South Street and South Crescent. Although Garlieston had been granted burgh of barony status, giving it the right to hold fairs and markets, that status was never given practical expression: the parish minister tells us in 1838 that none of those was held in the parish. The village hall is just out of shot on the right. The car parked in South Crescent indicates the location of the Galloway Arms Hotel, now the Ship Inn. In the Second World War the hotel continued the custom advertised in 1915 of catering for select guests, on this occasion senior army officers from London. The alleged reason for their presence was to check progress on the Mulberry Harbour experiments. Locally it was felt that their visits had more to do with the famous austerity-defying menus offered by the resourceful Mrs. Abbott.

Randolph Terrace was built in 1935-36 as part of the county council's drive to deal with the endemic problem of sub-standard housing in the landward areas of Wigtownshire. It was followed by two post-war developments, most notably Forteviot Gardens to the west of High Street. so that eventually half the houses in Garlieston were council-owned. The Terrace is named after Randolph, ninth Earl of Galloway. Although an Episcopalian, he was a notable benefactor of the Church of Scotland, making significant contributions to the building of new parish churches at Minnigaff, Penninghame (Newton Stewart), and Wigtown. He is commemorated by a monument in Newton Stewart at the western end of the Cree Bridge. Although not the owner of the ground, he was responsible for conserving the famous Cruggleton Arch, last easily visible relic of the castle that once stood there. The Austin Seven car and dark-suited gentleman appear to be used by the photographer as props since they appear in the picture of the village square above.

The local railway company's 1901 publication *Tours in Galloway* introduces its article on Garlieston with the heading " Favourite Watering Place" and declares "It has been steadily growing in favour as a summer resort". Among the attractions mentioned is the bowling club and the existence of a visitors' tournament with two trophies up for competition seems to confirm that claim. In fact the group appears to be a mixture of visitors and locals with two different dress codes in operation. The bowling green, established in the 1880s, occupies a prominent position on the seafront in South Crescent. Most Wigtownshire villages had a bowling green, but few could match Garlieston in its possession of a cricket club as well, perhaps the result of the proximity of Galloway House.

Tours in Galloway also cited the tennis club as one of the visitor attractions of Garlieston. The courts were situated at the head of the bay beyond North Crescent (Extreme Point), although a late 1940s brochure optimistically locates them in the centre of the village. Originally "splendid grass courts", they were later converted to blaes. In existence by 1901, the club was still operational in the 1950s, playing matches against some of the eight other clubs in Wigtownshire although not on the scale of the early days. At that time the club claimed to play a match or inter-club game every week during August and September. At five shillings per month visitors' fees were unlikely to act as a deterrent. The rope walk which provided an essential material for the shipyards was in this area.

Place names are a notoriously confusing subject to the amateur, the present instance being a prime example. Ruined Kirkmadrine Church on Penkiln Farm north of Garlieston is not to be equated with ruined Kirkmaiden Church south-west of Monreith on the shores of Luce Bay. It must also be distinguished from the remains of Kirkmaiden Church just north of the Mull of Galloway and certainly from Kirkmadrine Church with its early Christian stones south-west of Sandhead. Legend furnishes a connection between the two Kirkmaidens, although scholars might not concur, but not the two Kirkmadrines. Whatever their origins, the saint to whom the two churches were dedicated is unidentified; a Welsh female candidate called Modrun is not favoured by the experts. In the seventeenth century the Machars parish of Kirkmadrine was united with Cruggleton and Sorby parishes to form the present parish of Sorbie.

The "Two for the price of one" offer so beloved of supermarkets applies to the site of Sorbie Tower between that village and Garlieston for two castles are on offer. The less conspicuous is a motte, slightly unusual for its rectangular shape, partial terracing, and access to the summit by a flying bridge, features perhaps intended to impress the neighbours. It was replaced in the sixteenth century by the stone L-shaped tower house. This was for over 100 years the home of the Hannay or Ahanny family, also of Kirkdale in the Stewartry. The most remarkable Hannay was Patrick, who obtained a position as poet at the London court of fellow Scot King James VI and I, where he wrote elegant compliments to high-born ladies. Then in a radical career change he joined a Scots volunteer force to fight for the king of Bohemia, James's son-in-law, in Germany during the Thirty Years War.

Sorbie is a planned village established in the late eighteenth century by the seventh Earl of Galloway, who before his succession had founded nearby Garlieston. It was probably created as an industrial village as these cottages on the Garlieston road, which formed the original settlement, have the wide windows characteristic of weavers' cottages. Weaver James Walker, who established the damask industry here in the early 1790s, probably had financial backing from the earl. At any rate he aimed his product for the top end of the market, importing Dutch flax, processed for weaving at nearby Waulkmill. Sorbie produced double damask, the finest type, the elaborately embroidered linen cloth being woven in the workers' cottages. Its quickly acquired reputation for high quality was cemented when a suit of Sorbie damask won a national competition. After takeover by an Edinburgh firm the industry expanded to a workforce of 91 before changed economic circumstances brought about its demise around 1880. At least one example of Sorbie damask survives locally.

Old Sorbie Parish Church was completed in1755 although the date 1735 on the adjacent mausoleum of the earls of Galloway shows this was not the first church on the site. Sorbie residents' pride in being the kirk town of the parish dissolved into anger in 1875 when the Earl of Galloway as principal heritor decided that the required new church should be built in a more central position at Millisle, a mile west of Garlieston. One expression of local outraged feeling took the form of a satirical cartoon showing the church being removed in a wheelbarrow and depicting the kirk session as mere lackeys of the earl. Time may have healed the wounds but copies of the cartoon still exist locally. The name Sorbie, from the unflattering Norse "muddy settlement", confirms a tenth century Scandinavian presence in the area.

It was 1756 before Sorbie parish heritors (main landowners) belatedly and reluctantly, like their peers elsewhere, financed the provision of a parish school and salary for the master. But 40 years later the minister expressed satisfaction with the school's performance in a comment with a degree of political incorrectness: "All youth are educated according to their stations". His successor in 1838 showed a similar concern for the social aspects of education: "The increased facilities of education have certainly effected a corresponding increase in the knowledge and refinement of the people". In 1914 headmaster William Brown had already served at Sorbie for 24 years and was still ten years away from his retirement. Since the school roll in 1905 was 127, we can be sure that this picture is not of the entire school population. By 1962 Sorbie had a staff of three but today teachers and pupils have gone.

Whauphill's history is as a communications hub. The original clachan consisted of a handful of cottages beside an inn at a rural crossroads, but the village rose in importance with the opening of the Wigtownshire railway in 1875 when it became the railhead for Port William and the surrounding area with buses providing a regular linking service. The newer part of Whauphill beyond the trees with its shops and two-storey buildings a short distance from the station is the result of this increase in status. Perhaps it was the presence of the railway that led to the creation of a surprising amenity, a tarmac, floodlit curling rink situated just behind the photographer. Surprising also is the fact that Whauphill has a literary claim to fame, being the birthplace of a principal character in the work of fiction *Poor Things* by well known contemporary author and artist Alasdair Gray. In the book Dr Archie McCandless is the illegitimate son of a prosperous tenant farmer, whose Galloway Scots causes communication problems in Glasgow.

The antiquity of Kirkinner is attested by the discovery in the churchyard of two tenth century stone crosses carved in the style of the Whithorn school. They suggest that the clachan grew up round a chapel for the use of pilgrims on the route from Edinburgh to Whithorn and the shrine of St. Ninian, but the earlier name of the village, Carnesmoel, suggests an even earlier origin for it comes from British, the ancestor of Welsh, spoken in this area until the eighth century. However Kirkinner's most interesting resident belonged to the seventeenth century. Andrew Symson was Episcopalian minister of the parish for 23 years at the time of the bitter political-religious hostilities of that era. As Episcopalian minister of a staunchly Presbyterian area he found his pastoral duties undemanding and devoted his time to producing the first comprehensive account of the region, the classic *A Large Description of Galloway*. He was also more involved than he admitted in some of the most sensational events of that period.

With its wooden buildings and single platform Kirkinner Station was not designed to cater for a community of 1600 yet that is what happened during the Second World War when it became the station for RAF Wigtown, a Bomber Command training airfield less than two miles away. Local people never referred to the aerodrome by its official title; for them it was always Baldoon, the name of the farm on whose lands it was built. This dual nomenclature led, according to local lore, to a communication breakdown on at least one occasion when a new arrival alighted at Kirkinner Station and asked for directions to RAF Wigtown. He was emphatically assured by station staff that no such airfield existed in the vicinity. He would have to return to Carlisle and find transport to Wigton in Cumberland, where (presumably) he would find what he sought…

Bladnoch grew up where the road from Edinburgh and the north, the locally famous Old Edinburgh Road much favoured by Whithorn-bound pilgrims, crossed the river of that name by the lowest ford, later replaced by a bridge. The one in the picture dates from around 1860 and the builder demonstrated his workmanship by standing underneath it while a steam traction engine was driven across it. The clachan improbably blossomed into Wigtown's industrial suburb with a distillery (centre), a creamery, a coach-building business, an iron foundry, and, just outside the village, a farina mill. Facilities included three grocers' shops, two inns, and a bowling green. Recent investigation has proved that the river crossing was utilised well before medieval pilgrims patronised it: the site of a Roman fortlet has been discovered on the south bank of the river a little way upstream from the present village.

When brothers Thomas and John McClelland established their distillery at Bladnoch in 1817, the attraction was the abundant supply of river water used both as an ingredient in the whisky and to drive the wheel which originally powered the machinery. However, with the river tidal to just above the bridge it was necessary to extract the water half a mile further upstream. The lade bringing the water down to the distillery was known as "The Cut" and the name was eventually used for the narrow strip of wooded land between lade and river. The Cut was not only a pleasant walk but also gave access to the best place on the Bladnoch for swimming, Linghoor. For generations of local children "Going up The Cut" was synonymous with "Going swimming". After generations of water extraction from the river by the distillery, in an unintended reciprocal gesture in the 1960s the accidental opening of a valve discharged a large quantity of newly distilled spirit into the Bladnoch to the intense frustration of local residents.

Bladnoch Creamery, Wigtown. Copyright WGN 13. Raphael Tuck & Sons Ltd London.

Of the industries located in Bladnoch the creamery had the longest continuous existence and was the largest employer of labour. It was established in 1899 by The Scottish Co-operative Wholesale Society, who took advantage of an existing goods siding to gain access to the rail network. At first a conventional creamery, it acquired a margarine-manufacturing plant and became primarily although not solely a producer of Bluebell margarine, manufactured exclusively in Bladnoch. Bluebell seems to have been regarded by the SCWS as a status product for it was the theme of their display stand at the Glasgow Empire Exhibition of 1938. Creamery workers also took pride in the product as the factory concert party called themselves The Bluebell Entertainers. Bladnoch's boom years were in the 1950s and 1960s, when it was re-equipped with machinery which allowed it to manufacture "own brand" margarine for supermarkets, packaged and ready to go straight on to the shelves. The factory went on to 24-hour production for a time but economic circumstances changed and Bladnoch closed in the late 1980s.

FROM **Mrs. McCLŬMPHA,**
BLADNOCH, WIGTOWN, N.B.

Breeder of PURE-BRED POULTRY From Celebrated Laying Strains.

FIVE DIFFERENT BREEDS.

EGGS FOR HATCHING.   DAY OLD CHICKS.

CASH WITH ORDER.

DATE AS POST MARK.

Thos. P. Bethell, Boundary Place, Liverpool.

The firm of J. G. McClumpha was a long-established drapery business in Bladnoch with a large rural customer base for their clothes, manufactured by a team of tailors at one time numbering fourteen, based in several premises. The firm decided to diversify and acquired the farm of Kirkwaugh near the village. The supplying of poultry for commercial use seems to have been an offshoot of this and another example of the markets and opportunities opened up by the railways. In the 1901 edition of the local railway company's *Tours in Galloway* a list is given of people "willing to supply Butter, Eggs, Fruit, etc. by Passenger Train Direct to the Consumer". It contains twelve names, most of them of people living outside towns and villages but close to stations like Colfin, Palnure, and New Galloway. The McClumpha firm was eventually taken over by employee James Dewar.

Medieval Wigtown had the same roughly rectangular street plan as Whithorn but it has not been so completely preserved for in 1761 the council removed the West and East Ports. As the main street extended west (towards the photographer) and wheeled traffic increased, they were considered an obstruction to communication and "not of the smallest use to the place but rather a nuisance". One house on the north side of the West Port, almost in the centre of the picture, was retained but later demolished. In 1809 the widest part of the main street, long taken over by householders as a site for their domestic middens and a run for their hens, ducks, and other livestock, was enclosed and made into an ornamental garden. The trees on its perimeter are a conspicuous feature. Prominent also is the market cross, essential symbol of burgh status, which was erected in 1816 to replace a discarded older version, later re-erected beside its successor.

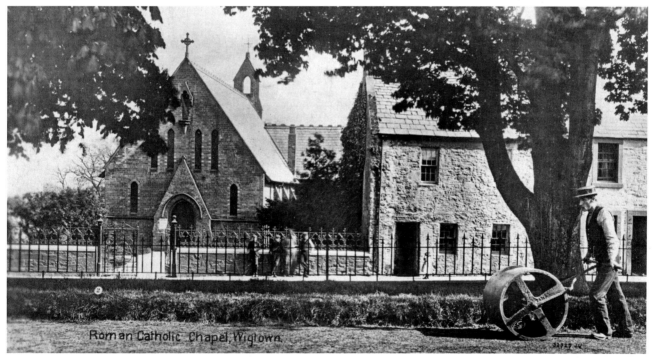

The Roman Catholic Sacred Heart chapel in South Main Street was built in 1879. Framing it are some of the trees lining the Square, the setting for a major controversy in 1875 when they had become the home of a number of crows, whose presence was claimed by some to be detrimental to the appearance of the royal burgh. At a council meeting it was proposed that both the crows and their nests should be destroyed. After an extremely animated debate the proposal was rejected but the incident reached the columns of the national newspapers. Clearly visible in the foreground are the railings "ornamental though not gaudy" erected at a cost of £150 to surmount the wall enclosing the gardens. In 1830 the latter were banished from the eastern end of the Square to make way for Wigtown Bowling Club. However once a year the bowlers had to give way to residents toasting the health of the reigning sovereign from the town's famous punchbowl, the gift of Queen Anne.

THE SQUARE, WIGTOWN.

The eastern end of Main Street (originally known as High Street) has been dominated for over 400 years by a succession of buildings carrying out functions vital to the running of the burgh and bearing names ranging from the original "tolbooth" to the present day "County Buildings", completed in 1862, its façade just visible on the right. The area in front of it is where major events in the life of the town traditionally take place. In the days when Wigtownshire was a separate parliamentary constituency returning two members it was also where election results were announced from the balcony. Sir Herbert Maxwell, who was first elected to parliament as member for the county constituency in 1880, vividly describes in his autobiography the scene here on that occasion: " the gusty square under the silent stars…the clamorous crowd…a halting speech from the successful candidate". The small house partly visible beyond the County Buildings was the home of Louis McGuffie V.C..

One of the functions of a tolbooth was to act as the burgh prison and to this end the 1747 replacement building had a suite of cells, this one on the ground floor and others on the upper floors. However, a Wigtown jailer's lot was not a happy one for a contract of 1799 laid down that he must also clean the streets as required by mowing the weeds and gathering the dung and rubbish. A further document of 1810 added to those duties the cleaning of the building, attending to the clock, and ringing the bell. All this was to be done without the unfortunate jailer neglecting his duties; in particular he was not to allow any drinking or rioting in the prison, an instruction that verges on stating the obvious as does the injunction that the jailer was to ensure the outer door was locked while he was inside the prison, the omission of which desirable precaution had led to several prisoners escaping.

The high street, much reduced in width, continued downhill past the north side of the tolbooth on the way to the church and the old harbour. It ended at the East Port just behind the spot where the photograph was taken. To the left of the modern church, built in 1850, are the ivy-covered remains of its predecessor of 1730, itself standing on the site of its medieval forerunner and incorporating sculptured stones of very early date. The adjoining churchyard contains two headstones traditionally associated with the story of the Wigtown martyrs. The war memorial includes the name of Louis McGuffie, posthumously awarded the Victoria Cross for feats of superlative courage in the Ypres Salient in 1917 during the First World War. Out of the picture, on the right, is the field which is the most likely site of the Dominican friary much patronised by King James IV on his pilgrimages to Whithorn and birthplace of that famous variety of apple, the Galloway pippin.

Built in 1935 and one of several housing developments in the town at this period, Jubilee Crescent commemorates the silver jubilee of King George V and Queen Mary. It is the only street name in Wigtown with royal connections in marked contrast to Newton Stewart where in the mid-nineteenth century most of the principal streets were re-christened with names of that kind. The same happened in Stranraer a century earlier. Isle of Whithorn also witnessed the disappearance of traditional street names but in this case with non-regal replacements. Perhaps the new names were felt to be more genteel or perhaps the Post Office demanded more precision but the result was the loss of evidence encapsulating the history of those places. Worst affected was the county town. Between 1841 and 1877 the historical name Wigton was replaced by the blander "Wigtown", apparently at the insistence of the Post Office on the grounds that confusion with Wigton in Cumbria was interfering with the efficient delivery of mail.

When the line of the Wigtownshire Railway was being planned, disagreement arose about the site for Wigtown Station. One option was to build it at the foot of the hill below the church and war memorial; the other favoured a site half-a mile to the south on the very outskirts of the town but near the harbour. The northern option was closer to the centre of town (600 yards instead of 900) but the gradient from the station was 1 in 21 whereas that from the southern option (the Maidland option, after the nearby farm) was 1 in 30. The Maidland option was chosen, putting Wigtown among the majority of local stations in its long walk from town to train. It was the first station on the new line to open for business in April, 1875. Here the operator of the line, the legendary Thomas Wheatley, had the workshop where he performed the technical miracles of improvisation and adaptation required of a tiny budget.

Music seems to have flourished in Wigtown. The splendid uniforms of the Burgh Brass Band contrasted with the suits and caps of their earlier days. The band was still in existence after the Second World War, as was the Wigtown and Bladnoch Pipe Band, the second name of the title being vital as the big drummer hailed from that village. The most famous musician associated with the town is the late John Mason, founder and first conductor of The Scottish Fiddle Orchestra. Not a native of Wigtown he moved there as a schoolboy in the early 1950s and soon established himself as a leading figure in the local and later national music scene. Given his astonishing skill and versatility as a musician it is surprising that in youth he had a hearing problem. The imposing figure of Bandmaster McCredie in the front row is flanked on his right by the remarkable Provost Shaw, dominant figure in local life in the 1920s and 30s, possessor of three professional degrees, in Divinity, Law, and Medicine, friend of Robert Louis Stevenson and Sir Arthur Conan Doyle.

The main hill sheep rearing area in Wigtownshire is the Moors. Kirkcowan stands on the edge of that district with a fast-flowing stretch of the Tarff Water close by. The resulting opportunity to establish a woollen industry was taken in the late eighteenth century by Robert Milroy, the son of a local farmer, who had served an apprenticeship as a dyer. His original mill was rebuilt and extended several times by succeeding members of the Milroy family, who remained involved in the business until it eventually closed about 1950. Their Waulk Mill can be seen on the left. Its main products were blankets and plaiding; at the outbreak of war in 1939 it turned out large quantities of blankets as bedding for evacuee children. In 1839 the workforce numbered 39 and in the 1880s water power was supplemented by steam power. The other mill, The Tarff Mills, on the right, was established in the mid-nineteenth century by the Armstrongs, a Borders family, but eventually taken over by the Milroys.

As "Armstrongs' Mills" (as they are locally known) are on the opposite side of the Tarff from the village, access to them is by "a picturesque old bridge". According to an 1838 report the Tarff provided more than the motive power for the machinery; the softness of the water made it well suited for use in the dyeing process. However, during periods of drought the level of the Tarff became too low to allow the mills to operate efficiently and steps had been taken to deal with the problem. A few miles upstream a channel fitted with a sluice gate had been cut between Loch Ronald and the river. When the latter reached a low level, the local postman was asked to convey a message by word of mouth to a farmer's wife living close to Loch Ronald. The lady then opened the sluice gate, the water level quickly rose, and normal working resumed at the mills. In recognition of her valued services she received a pair of blankets annually.

At the south end of Kirkcowan the two rows of cottages, Neilson Place and Milroy Terrace, gable on to the street on the extreme right, were built by the mill owners of the latter name to house their workers. In the centre are the remains of the old parish church built in 1658 and in use for almost 200 years. The origin of the name of the village is the subject of some speculation, but it would most suitably mean "The church of Eoghan". The gentleman was an early fifth century Irish bishop who had had the misfortune to be captured by pirates and sold into slavery in Brittany, in which situation he was forced to work in a mill. Kirkcowan could not wish for a more appropriate saint to whom to have its church dedicated.

"There cam a strange wight to our town-en": Kirkcowan is the setting for William Nicholson's great poem, based on folk lore, *The Brownie of Blednoch*. That the Blednoch of the title is the river that flows past the village and not the clachan of that name several miles downstream is very clear from the occurrence in the poem of three other place names in the vicinity. In the early days of the mills this street echoed every morning except Sunday to the sound of a man blowing a trumpet. As the mill workers had no clocks or watches and had to rise early, his job was to waken them up. His nickname was "Toot". In 1875 the *Guide to Wigtownshire* claimed Kirkcowan had "a plain, homely, Scottish aspect", a view confirmed by this 1906 scene. Thirty years later the village had seventeen shops most of them here in Main Street. Sadly these halcyon days are past.

Like the south end of Main Street, the north extremity is terminated by a church, this time the present parish church built in 1834 to replace its seventeenth century predecessor. A name famously associated with it is that of John Crozier, who for 60 years of last century from the age of twenty was precentor and organist as well as the inspiration of the village's vibrant musical scene. In a strange juxtaposition of the sacred and the profane, 200 yards up the Stranraer road in a clump of trees is the site of an old inn temptingly named Stay the Voyage. In the boom years of smuggling around 1800 it was a favourite resort of smugglers en route from the landing places on the east side of Luce Bay across the moors to Ayrshire and Edinburgh. All contraband routes from that shore led to Kirkcowan, where other competitors for the smugglers' lucrative business were the Thatch Inn and Nancy Shepherd's hostelry at Kiltersan near the present Halfway House.

While the occasion and location of this event are uncertain, the dress styles on display are quite irresistible. The attire of the gentleman on the extreme right is particularly noteworthy. It is possible that this is the annual sports day of the Kirkcowan Oddfellows, a major event in the village calendar. The Brownie of Bladnoch Lodge was established in 1872 and was one of eleven such groups in Wigtownshire. The Oddfellows combined the functions of a social club and a friendly society. The location is probably Ballgreen Park football ground on the south-west of the village, home of the redoubtable Tarff Rovers. The modest wooden pavilion on the right was burned down and replaced. When Partick Thistle FC visited on Scottish Cup business in the 1950s, their manager was appalled by the accommodation and facilities and petitioned vigorously for the game to be relocated.

Kirkcowan Railway Station on the Dumfries-Stranraer line was located rather incongruously in a field some distance from the village. An evocative glimpse of it is provided by Ian Niall (John McNeillie) in his *A Galloway Childhood*: "the little office at the end of the white-painted fence" and the "stationmaster and ticket collector…busy manhandling (milk) churns" in a commendable display of multi-tasking. However, the station almost had greatness thrust upon it. When the "Machars Railway" was being planned in 1871, Sir David Dunbar of Mochrum Park near Kirkcowan proposed that it should branch off the main line at Kirkcowan instead of Newton Stewart, leave out the county town of Wigtown altogether, and head south for Whauphill. The proposal was heavily defeated and the station, bereft of possible junction status, had to content itself with the occasional visit from the Marquess of Bute and his family travelling to and from the family residence at Old Place of Mochrum.

Glaisnick Bridge on the River Bladnoch was not intended for leisure strollers and sightseeing but to give the residents, particularly the schoolchildren, of the two Glaisnicks on the east side of the river quicker access to Kirkcowan by way of Barhoise Mill. Under its alternative name of Glaisnick ("Glashnoch") Mill, the latter is mentioned in *The Brownie of Blednoch* as is the nearby Linn of Barhoise waterfall, which Aiken-drum the brownie offers to leap. Most place names in Wigtownshire are Gaelic, but the two rivers, Bladnoch and Tarff, that delineate the parish of Kirkcowan have names derived from the earliest language known to have been spoken in south-west Scotland, British, the ancestor of Welsh and Cornish and forerunner of Gaelic. It seems that the earliest articulate inhabitants lived in an area we now regard as moorland, perhaps an indication of a change in climate and so vegetation.

Newton Stewart's former industrial sector at the north end of the town occupies the bottom right-hand quadrant of the picture. It was established around 1790 by local-boy-made-good Sir William Douglas from the Moss of Cree. At a cost of £20,000 he built "a large work for the spinning of cotton by mill machinery" using water power from the River Cree. The horseshoe weir that fed the lade is still visible. Sadly the venture failed and the mill became derelict. It was eventually bought by the Earl of Galloway, who used it as a dressed stone quarry for houses and farm buildings on his estate. The resulting "almost vacant site", as an 1874 writer described it, is seen here. However by 1908 the firm of Milroy had erected on the site tweed mills, which became the famous Cree Mills, producers of mohair products. Firm and buildings have both disappeared and housing now occupies the site. The chimney by the river almost in the centre belonged to a brewery, now private housing.

Newton Stewart eventually squeezed out of the narrow strip between river and high ground to the west and expanded south along the Wigtown road. The two-storey houses in the centre foreground are standard inter-war municipal issue but the bungalows of the same era on the other side of the road, together with five at Windsor Terrace, represent pioneering technology for they are constructed of prefabricated steel and were manufactured by the Weir group, who thought them sufficiently important to send company chairman Lord Weir to the formal opening in 1925. Time has proved the popularity of "the steel houses". Across the foreground runs the embankment carrying the Dumfries-Stranraer railway, route of the legendary Irish boat train "The Paddy" but closed in 1963. Just left of centre is the octagonal livestock auction mart, built in 1895 by a group of local businessmen and farmers. Nowadays it enjoys national fame as the venue for sales of Blackface sheep at record-breaking prices.

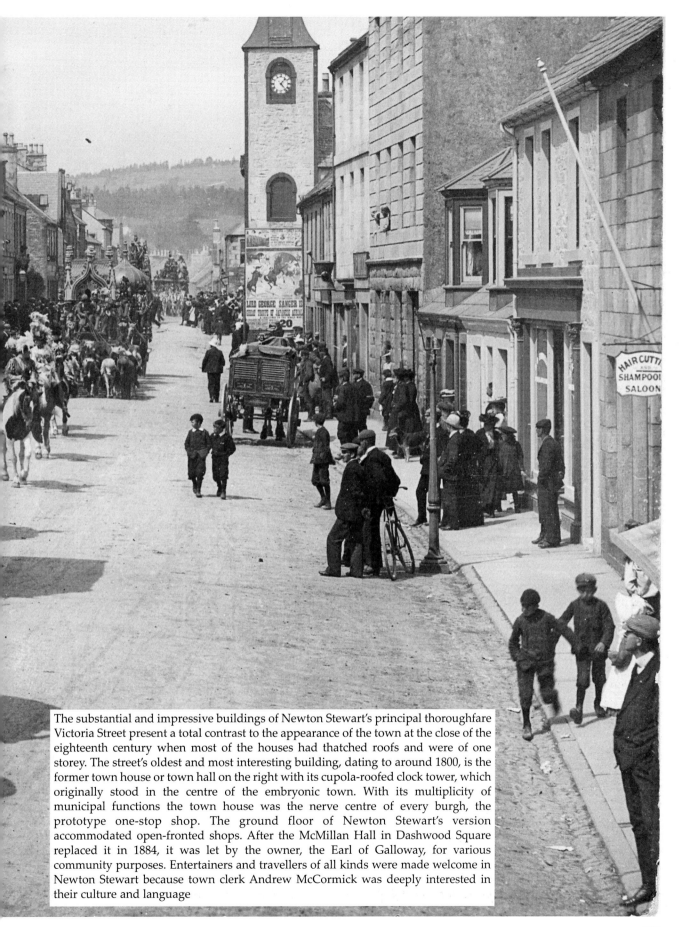

The substantial and impressive buildings of Newton Stewart's principal thoroughfare Victoria Street present a total contrast to the appearance of the town at the close of the eighteenth century when most of the houses had thatched roofs and were of one storey. The street's oldest and most interesting building, dating to around 1800, is the former town house or town hall on the right with its cupola-roofed clock tower, which originally stood in the centre of the embryonic town. With its multiplicity of municipal functions the town house was the nerve centre of every burgh, the prototype one-stop shop. The ground floor of Newton Stewart's version accommodated open-fronted shops. After the McMillan Hall in Dashwood Square replaced it in 1884, it was let by the owner, the Earl of Galloway, for various community purposes. Entertainers and travellers of all kinds were made welcome in Newton Stewart because town clerk Andrew McCormick was deeply interested in their culture and language

The gentleman at the door of 42 Victoria Street is maybe W.M. Kelly himself although his attire indicates he is bound for a field sports venue rather than his office or the courtroom. In practice in the late 1920s, he faced formidable competition from well known local figure McCormick, who had an unrivalled knowledge of the Galloway hills and was the author of several books on his two great enthusiasms. Further legal competition was provided by A.S. Morton, burgh prosecutor, expert in local history and antiquities, and author of the magisterial *Galloway and the Covenanters*. Reflected in Mr Kelly's left-hand window from a shop opposite or parked van is the name of prominent local business, McDonalds, furniture makers and upholsterers.

An event in Newton Stewart in June, 1921, has strong echoes of one of the great moments in modern Scottish religious history. In Edinburgh in 1843 a large number of dissenting ministers and elders left the Church of Scotland General Assembly being held in St. Andrew's Church in George Street and walked in procession down Dundas Street to Tanfield Hall at Canonmills to found a new church, the Free Church of Scotland. Almost 80 years later in Newton Stewart the entire congregation, evicted from Creebridge United Free Church, also in a bitter internecine dispute, walked through the town in procession to their hall, effectively creating a new congregation. In both national and local cases the dispute was eventually resolved. In a symbolic moment the ousted congregation is crossing John Rennie's 1813 Cree Bridge from Kirkcudbrightshire, where Creebridge is situated, into Wigtownshire and their new home. The disputed church, which underwent several name changes, eventually became a guest house and is now demolished.

It is appropriate that the girls of the Douglas Circle are collecting for the Children's League of Pity for their school was originally a charitable institution "The Samuel Douglas Free School", established by the gentleman of that name. Samuel Douglas was a native of Penninghame parish and latterly owner of a Jamaican tea- and coffee plantation probably part of the Douglas family import-export business in which cousin William was a leading participant. His school was for the education of around twelve " Indigent children of honest and respectable Parents" born in the parishes of Penninghame or Kirkmabreck, the

latter his parents' birthplace. Although he died in South Carolina in 1791, his school was not opened at the north end of Newton Stewart until 1833. In addition to the twelve foundationers, the Douglas also took fee-paying pupils both day and residential, catering mainly for boys. Boarding pupils attended the parish church on Sundays wearing Eton suits and tall hats, quite a contrast to the dress of the Douglas Circle.

This staff group probably represents the popular image of the Douglas Academy; in fact it became an all-girls school only in 1891 when it and the town's other endowed school, the Ewart Institute, came under the same administration, the Ewart thenceforth catering exclusively for boys. The Douglas High School, as it was now known, still catered for boarders "to whose health, happiness and advancement every care is given". Some day pupils commuted daily by train or stayed in digs in Newton Stewart from Monday to Friday. A high standard of dress was expected: no girl was permitted to leave the campus unless wearing hat and gloves. It may be the strict regime was the consequence of headmistress Miss Millan having been a student at Dresden University. In 1922 the Douglas and the Ewart were amalgamated and handed over to the Wigtownshire Education authority. Of the Douglas building's later numerous roles the strangest was when it was used to audition for local extras for the 1970s cult film *The Wicker Man*.

Newton Stewart Pipe Band against the impressive background of Pennnghame Parish Church. The black and white photograph makes identification of their tartan impossible but it would be appropriate if it were one of the Stewart varieties for Newton Stewart was founded by William Stewart, a younger son of the Earl of Galloway, who granted the first feu charter in 1701. In the modern era local pipe bands have an additional choice of tartan : around 1948 John Hannay, a native of Minnigaff resident in London, devised a Galloway tartan in two versions, the Hunting Galloway and the Dress Galloway. Stranraer and District Pipe Band took advantage of the new opportunity by adopting the blue-and-red Dress Galloway, which has proved the more popular of the two.

Newton Stewart Boys' Brigade company in the inter-war years was a formidably well equipped and variously talented group with its own in-house pipe band and some members presumably proficient with the rifles they carried, evidence that the company had affiliated to the army cadet scheme. Company captain was the imposing figure of Rev. Brown Douglas, minister in Newton Stewart for 40 years, officiating in three different churches. The manse Old English Sheepdog was one of a pair which the Brown Douglases kept in a remarkable exercise in self-sufficiency surely dear to the heart of today's conservation lobby. Mrs. Brown Douglas retained all the combings from her meticulous dog-grooming and had them spun and woven into cloth, which was then made into suits for her. In the immediate post-war years the most prominent youth group was the Minnigaff scout troop, consisting mainly of boys from Newton Stewart.

The location of the Devil's Wood poses a stiff problem but clues in the picture suggest it may be on the Newton Stewart-Girvan road between Penninghame House and Clachaneasy, where the road runs close to the stretch of the river known as the Loch of Cree. Certainly a supernatural tale is associated with the ruins of St. Ninian's Chapel at the roadside just beyond the Penninghame House policies. Allegedly one pitch-dark winter morning a succession of pedestrians on their way to work were violently assaulted here by an unseen and seemingly intangible adversary. A hurried request to a local minister for assistance brought the reply that they had encountered an evil spirit called Makkin and the minister was hurrying to conduct a ceremony of exorcism. Just then the district midwife (the howdie) arrived on the scene carrying a lantern, which revealed the assailant was a donkey tethered to the roadside with its rear hooves in the attack position.

As its Gaelic name confirms, the River Cree forms the eastern boundary of Wigtownshire from the estuary to Bargrennan. With a strong dash of imagination the local claim that in its meanderings it writes its own name could almost be accepted. However the same meanderings rule it out as a significant commercial highway. The head of navigation is Carty Port just under two miles from Newton Stewart, which, before the railway arrived, was used by vessels of up to 45 tons bringing in lime and coal and some manufactured goods. *The (New) Statistical Account* of 1841 surprisingly claimed that with spring tides the Liverpool steamer had called (with some difficulty) at Carty. At the very mouth of the river commercial traffic was at one time maintained by a small, undecked, sailing boat which provided a once-a-day (twice in summer) ferry service between Creetown and Wigtown. As proof of the service's importance the arrival at Wigtown of the "Ferry Packet" was announced by the blowing of a horn.

Cruives O'Cree, Newton Stewart.